Key Irish Women Writers

Series Editors: Kathryn Laing and Sinéad Mooney

1. Clíona Ó Gallchoir, *Maria Edgeworth*
2. Heather Ingman, *Elizabeth Bowen*
3. Aintzane Legarreta Mentxaka, *Kate O'Brien*
4. Eibhear Walshe, *Jane Wilde*

Advance acclaim

'This study of Jane Wilde's life and work is welcome as part of current efforts to restore her to her rightful place in Irish literary history'.
    – **Heather Ingman**, author of *Elizabeth Bowen* (Key Irish Women Writers Series), *Irish Women's Fiction: From Edgeworth to Enright, A Modern Literary Life. Elizabeth Bowen, A Memoir* and co-editor with Clíona Ó Gallchoir of *A History of Modern Irish Women's Literature.*

Jane Wilde

I dedicate this to
Saul Perez
with love and thanks.

Jane Wilde

Eibhear Walshe

EER
Edward Everett Root, Publishers, Brighton, 2023.

EER
Edward Everett Root, Publishers, Co. Ltd.,
Atlas Chambers, 33 West Street, Brighton, Sussex, BN1 2RE, England.
Details of our overseas agents in America, Australia, China, Europe, and Japan, and how to buy our books are given on our website.
www.eerpublishing.com

edwardeverettroot@yahoo.co.uk

Key Irish Women Writers series, volume 4.

© Eibhear Walshe, 2023.

First published in England 2023.

This edition © Edward Everett Root Publishers, 2023.

ISBN: 978-1-913087-43-2 paperback
ISBN: 978-1-913087-44-9 hardback
ISBN: 978-1-913087-45-6 ebook

Eibhear Walshe has asserted his right to be identified as the owner of the copyright of this Work in accordance with the Copyright, Designs and Patents Act 1988 as the owner of this Work.

All rights reserved. No part of this publication may be reproduced, stored in a retrieval system or transmitted in any form or by any means, electronic, mechanical, photocopying, recording or otherwise, without the prior permission of the copyright owner.

Cover and book production by Pageset Limited, High Wycombe, Bucks.

Contents

Acknowledgements ix
Chronology. xi
Introduction: The Salon in Merrion Square. 1
Chapter One: Education (1821–1845) 13
Chapter Two: Inventing Speranza (1845–1851) 21
    Writing the Famine. 30
    The Trial of *The Nation* 53
    Daniel O'Connell 58
    Sidonia The Sorceress (1849). 62
Chapter Three: Merrion Square (1851–1879) 67
    Lotten von Kræmer. 74
    Driftwood from Scandinavia (1884) 78
    The Mary Travers Trial. 91
    The Death of William Wilde and Aftermath 102
Chapter Four: London (1879–1896). 109
    Ancient Legends, Mystic Charms, and Superstitions of Ireland
       (1887). 114
    Ancient Cures, Charms, and Usages of Ireland (1890) 122
    Notes on Men, Women, and Books (1891) 128
    Social Studies (1893) 139
Conclusion 151
Bibliography 153
Index. 157

The author

EIBHEAR WALSHE lectures in the School of English at University College Cork in Ireland where he is Director of Creative Writing. He publishes fiction, memoir, literary criticism and biography, and his books include *Kate O'Brien: A Writing Life* (2006), *Oscar's Shadow: Wilde and Ireland* (2012), and *A Different Story: the Writings of Colm Toibin* (2013). His childhood memoir, *Cissie's Abattoir* (2009), was broadcast on RTE's 'Book on One.' His novel, *The Diary of Mary Travers* (2014), was shortlisted for the Kerry Group Novel of the Year Award in 2015 and longlisted for the 2016 International Dublin Literary Award. He was associate editor, with Catherine Marshall, of *Modern Ireland in 100 Artworks* (2016), edited by Fintan O'Toole and shortlisted for the Irish Book Award. His other novels include *The Trumpet Shall Sound* (2019), longlisted for the 2021 International Dublin Literary Award and *The Last Day at Bowen's Court* (2020) and he edited *The Selected Writings of Speranza and William Wilde* (2020).

Acknowledgments

In working on this study of Jane Wilde I was greatly assisted by the scholarship and kindness of Eleanor Fitzsimons, Donald O'Driscoll, Merlin Holland, Noreen Doody, Heather Bryant, Kathryn Laing and Sinéad Mooney. I would like to thank my colleagues in the School of English in University College Cork and in particular Claire Connolly and Lee Jenkins. I would also like to thank my colleagues on the Project, "INTRUTHS 2: Articulations of Individual and Communal Vulnerabilities in Contemporary Irish Writing," supported by the Spanish Ministry of Science and Innovation, for all their help and insights into the silencing of Speranza, dealt with in my essay for the forthcoming volume, *Narratives of the Unspoken in Contemporary Irish Fiction* (2023), edited by M. Teresa Caneda-Cabrera and José Carregal-Romero.

I want to thank the College of Arts, Celtic Studies and Social Sciences for a research grant to carry out my work.

Chronology

1801. The Act of Union comes into effect, abolishing the Irish parliament.
1803. A rebellion led by Robert Emmet and other United Irishmen against British rule. Emmet and the other leaders are executed.
1821. Jane Elgee (Speranza) born in Dublin on 21st December.
1823. The Catholic Association is founded to campaign for equal rights for Catholics.
1828. Daniel O'Connell becomes MP for County Clare.
1829. Catholic Emancipation is granted, allowing Catholics to hold any political office, including that of MP.
1840. Daniel O'Connell forms the National Association, aimed at repeal of the Union.
1845. The start of the Great Famine. The potato crop is completely destroyed. Thomas Davis's funeral takes place in Dublin, inspiring Jane Elgee's first foray into poetry.
1846. Jane Elgee sends poems into *The Nation* under the name Speranza, Italian for hope.
1847. Soup kitchens established and outdoor famine relief authorised, but only for those who held a quarter acre of land or less. Jane Elgee publishes her Famine poems in *The Nation*.
1848. The Young Ireland revolt led by William Smith O'Brien. Its leaders are captured and sentenced to transportation for life. She becomes editor of *The Nation*.

1849. The *Nation* trial for treason and sedition takes place and Jane Elgee's writings come under scrutiny.
1850. Speranza's translation of Lamartine's *History of the Girondins* published.
William Wilde publishes *The Beauties of the Boyne*, reviewed by Jane Elgee in the *Dublin University Magazine*.
1851. Jane and William marry and settle into their first home at Westland Row in Dublin.
1852. Willie, their eldest son, born. Jane Wilde publishes her translation of *The Glacier Land*. William publishes *Irish Popular Superstitions*.
1854. Oscar, their second son, born.
1857. Their daughter Isola born.
1858. The family move to Merrion Square.
1858. The Fenian Brotherhood (Irish Republican Brotherhood) formed.
1864. Jane Wilde publishes *Poems by Speranza,* William knighted. The Mary Travers case takes place.
1867. Isola dies. William Wilde publishes *Lough Corrib*.
1867. The Fenian Rising.
1869. The Church of Ireland is disestablished.
1873. Isaac Butt founds the Home Rule Movement.
1875. Charles Stewart Parnell is elected as MP for County Meath.
1876. William Wilde dies.
1878. Jane Wilde publishes her pamphlet *The American Irish*.
1879. Jane Wilde moves to London. The Irish National Land League is founded, Charles Stewart Parnell is made president.
1880. Jane Wilde completes and publishes William's last book, *Memoir of Gabriel Beranger*.
1882. The Gaelic Athletic Association formed.
1884. *Driftwood from Scandinavia* published.
1887. *Ancient Legends, Mystic Charms, and Superstitions of Ireland.*

1890. *Ancient Cures, Charms and Usages.*
1891. *Notes on Men, Women, and Books.*
1893. *Social Studies.*
1895. Oscar Wilde trials in London. Oscar committed to prison.
1896. Jane Wilde dies in London.

INTRODUCTION

The Salon in Merrion Square

Broadly speaking, when a carefully and selectively constructed national canon once functioned to cover or mask the fracturing that frequently characterises the relationship between place and identity in Ireland, contemporary scholarship now actively explores how writing has grown in precisely those cracks and fissures.[1]

On a November evening in 2019, in a Georgian house in the centre of Dublin, a literary salon was revived after more than one hundred and forty years. This revival was to celebrate the legacy of the Irish poet Jane Wilde. Back in the 1860s, every Saturday afternoon at 4pm, Jane Wilde, one of Ireland's leading writers, opened her doors to Dublin's intellectual and scientific community. Novelists, professors, politicians, and translators flocked to her house at Number One, Merrion Square in the centre of Dublin to drink tea, read their works, and talk politics. Now, in 2019, in this new iteration, young Irish artists and writers came to read their poems, play Irish music, and sing rebel songs in the large upper rooms of this same Georgian house, at the same time, Saturday afternoon between four and eight. The house is now occupied by a private third-level institution, The American College. They had organised this free event, to connect a general

---

1. Introduction, *A History of Modern Irish Women's Literature*. Edited by Heather Ingman and Clíona Ó'Gallchoir (Cambridge: Cambridge University Press, 2018), p. 4.

audience with the literary history of the house and of the Wilde family, and to showcase the work of young Irish writers and singers. Many of the young writers told the audience that they had never heard of this salon before this. More than that, they knew very little about the woman who used to host these gatherings. Her name was somewhat familiar to these writers, but her poems were not. Each one of these young writers, however, went to the trouble of finding her poems wherever they could, to celebrate her legacy and connect with her imaginatively. The woman who once lived here, a committed Irish nationalist poet would have relished the energy and the enthusiasm of the young writers and the singers, and the Irish rebel songs they sang.

The selectively-constructed canon of Irish writing has, until recently, excluded Jane Wilde from any serious consideration as a figure of significance in the history of nineteenth-century cultural life. Most of Jane Wilde's writings have been lost within the cracks and fissures of Irish literary history. My intention in this study is to reclaim her writings, outline her impressive literary achievements and consider the illuminating contradictions of her social and cultural assumptions, especially her complex views on feminism. She was an advocate of women's rights who often saw the domestic figure of the wife and mother as the enemy of creativity and, in this, embodied much of the ambivalence of the Victorian era. In her lifetime, Jane Wilde was a celebrated poet, an important cultural influence, and her writings bore witness to moments of real drama and tension in her society. In her poetry, she engaged with these moments and with the pressing political debates and controversies of Ireland with originality and passion. Her writings provide a unique perspective on that time and those debates. In this study I explore the versatility of her creativity and of her intellectual preoccupations and scholarship. In her lifetime, Dublin-born, middle-class Protestant Jane Wilde (1896) was a vocal supporter of Irish nationalism in her poetry and in her essays. In addition, she was a key witness to the desolation of the

Irish Famine, a keen-eyed social commentator and radical in her desire for social justice. When her salon was in full glory during the 1860s, Ireland was still part of the British Empire. She had opposed British rule in her writings to such a degree that, at one point, she had nearly been thrown into prison herself for inciting armed revolt against the British administration in Dublin by writing 'Oh! For a hundred thousand muskets glittering brightly in the light of heaven, and the monumental barricades stretching across each of our noble streets, made desolate by England – circling around that doomed Castle.'[2] Yet she attended events in Dublin Castle throughout her life, where her husband William was knighted by the Lord Lieutenant. She managed to live within this apparently contradictory social sphere, even commenting on this with relish in letters to her friends. Many of the contemporary young Irish writers in the 2019 salon were unclear as to what to call her. Like many public figures, Jane Wilde invented and then reinvented herself several times during her career and her names reflect this. She began life as Jane Frances Elgee, the daughter of a Dublin lawyer, but she became the poet Speranza, also changing her name to Jane Francesca Elgee. Calling herself by an Italianate pen name was deliberate, implying that the name Elgee came from Alighieri, distantly related to Dante. This was not factually true, but for Jane Wilde, the process of self-invention included the creation of a kind of personal legend. For the purposes of this study, I will call her Jane Wilde, the name she used when publishing her books and her collected poems.

Her interest in self-invention included a recognition of the effectiveness of her own visual presentation. A tall, handsome, confident woman, she took care to dress well, using vivid colours, beautiful fabrics, and striking ornaments to connect with the mythology of her country. A performance of self and an

---

2. Originally published in *The Nation,* July 1848. See Eibhear Walshe, *Selected Writings of Speranza and William Wilde* (Liverpool: Liverpool University Press, 2020), p. 53.

identification with the idea of Ireland as a spiritualised entity was part of Jane Wilde's public persona and was successful within her own lifetime. Afterwards, it was used against her in some of the more hostile biographies, like that of Terence de Vere White, who referred to her as a pantomime queen.[3]

Famous in her lifetime, she became somewhat infamous, or – perhaps to put it more accurately – ridiculed, in the years after her death. Like many Irish women writers, much of her writing has been lost and is now out of print. Core to this project is a recognition of the fact that her scholarship as a translator, literary critic and travel writer has been neglected, that her poems are now broadly unknown and her posthumous afterlife problematic. There is a troubling sense that Jane Wilde was not simply forgotten in the years after her death in 1896. Whenever Jane Wilde was remembered in the twentieth century, it was as a parody of herself. During her lifetime, she played the role of the poet in public, like her hero Byron. But, unlike Byron, she paid the price for this.

One of the most damaging aspects to her silenced or damaged afterlife was a concentration on her appearance, her self-invention, her unreliability as a narrator of her own life and her artistic persona. Snide descriptions of her clothes, her regal air, and her role as Ireland's martyr queen were linked to a deploring of the supposed role she played in her son's downfall. White, while acknowledging that she and her husband 'had acquired something of the inevitability and pathos of the routine vaudeville act', perpetuated much of this prejudice by writing that William Wilde's enthusiasms 'had an intellectual basis, while his wife's were emotional: they went with her craving for sensation.'[4] Nonetheless, White does profess some respect for her: 'To her, he [Oscar] owed most of his qualities, for good and ill.'[5] At the

---

3. Terence de Vere White, *The Parents of Oscar Wilde* (London: Hodder & Stoughton, 1967), p. 17.
4. Ibid., p. 17.
5. Ibid., p. 17.

same time, he also depicts the family as tainted by inordinate sentimentality: 'Whatever strain was in the Wilde family that led to sexual disorder and disaster.'[6]

In terms of the decline of her literary and intellectual reputation, it was not a case of simple neglect. It is more the fact that Jane Wilde came to be remembered with contempt. Why?

The public disgrace of her son Oscar was profoundly damaging for her afterlife because of the widespread homophobia it provoked, which rebounded onto her supposed role in causing his 'sexual disorder.' Oscar Wilde always made it clear that he had learnt the discipline of writing and scholarship from both his mother and from his father. In *De Profundis* he wrote 'She and my father had bequeathed me a name they had made noble and honoured, not merely in literature, art, archaeology, and science, but in the public history of my own country, in its evolution as a nation.'[7] He had also learnt the art of the performance of a public selfhood from his mother and it had enabled his public persona and enhanced his literary reputation until he became implicated in the most public of homosexual scandals in 1895. Jane Wilde supported her son all through his downfall and faced down the vicious public opprobrium. However, her loyalty to her son and her perceived influence dealt her own literary reputation a fatal blow. I have argued in my book, *Oscar's Shadow*,[8] that the assumed connection between her own unconventional and bohemian persona and her son's criminalised sexuality damaged Jane Wilde's reputation profoundly. She was scapegoated and accused of perverting his sexual identity because of her own anti-bourgeois impulses and stances. In addition, a homophobic and misogynist Victorian sexual discourse blamed her overpowering maternal influence as the cause of his homosexuality, that her lack of conventional 'mothering' had somehow unmanned Oscar.

---
6. Ibid., p. 17.
7. Oscar Wilde, *De Profundis* (Harmondsworth: Penguin, 1986), p. 141.
8. Eibhear Walshe, *Oscar's Shadow* (Cork: Cork University Press, 2011).

(This is despite abundant biographical evidence of her closeness to all her children during their early years and her support for both her adult sons' careers).

One of the most revealing stories or myths in the afterlife of Jane Wilde came on the night of her death. When she was dying in London, poor and miserable, her beloved son was locked up in prison and was unable to visit her. She died without seeing him again, and his wife Constance travelled from her exile in Switzerland to break the news to him, knowing how sorrowful he would be. When his wife told him the news, his reaction was, "I knew it already." The night she had died he had sensed she was in his cell. She was dressed for out-of-doors, and he asked her to take off her hat and cloak and sit down. But she shook her head sadly and vanished.'[9] It has always struck me as significant that she was, for once, silent in his account of the last encounter with her beloved son. It was a premonition of what was to come. In the twentieth century, her fluent and generous voice was silenced. Another version of her life and of her character would overwhelm her own voice.

Oscar Wilde's respect for his mother's scholarship, her learning and her intellectual rigour was merited, and he made this abundantly clear in his letters and in all of his warm, affectionate, and supportive interactions with his mother. Moreover, he was not alone in this. In her lifetime, the Irish patriot, Charles Gavan Duffy called her 'A substantial force in Irish politics, and a woman of genius.'[10] W. B. Yeats, for another, celebrated her life and her work and was a close and admiring friend. Despite the damage to her reputation, her collections of Irish folk tales were in circulation in Ireland in the twentieth century, as well as a handful of her Famine poems.

However, the broader corpus of her work, her essays and translations, fell out of print, and her reputation as a scholar and a

---

9. Joy Melville, *Mother of Oscar* (London: John Murray 1994), p. 265.
10. Charles Gavan Duffy, *In Two Hemispheres* (Dublin: Unwin, 1898), p. 75.

writer was compromised. Much of this was due to one biographical source, another Dublin writer, George Bernard Shaw. Shaw was usually a generous and good-natured friend but, in the case of Jane Wilde, he did considerable damage to the reputation of someone who, in his own words, 'was nice to me in London during the desperate days between my arrival in 1876 and my first earnings of an income from my pen in 1885.'[11] Shaw sent his friend Frank Harris an account of Jane Wilde in her final years in London which blamed her for Oscar's downfall and his sexuality. He attended her literary salon in London, ungenerously calling them 'desperate affairs',[12] and repaid her kindness with his misogynistic theories about her malign genetic influence on her son. Shaw offers a bizarre explanation for Wilde's so-called aberrant sexuality by theorising that Jane herself was suffering from an abnormal physical condition called gigantism: 'I never saw Lady Wilde's feet but her hands were enormous and never went straight to their aim when they grasped anything but minced about, feeling for it. And the gigantic splaying of her palm was produced in her lumbar region.'[13] It was implied that Wilde had inherited her physical abnormality, remade somehow as homosexuality. Shaw provides no medical proof for this theory, apart from the evidence of his own eyes,[14] and no other contemporary account mentions this condition. Thus, it is arguable that Shaw enabled a century of homophobic hostility towards Jane Wilde from subsequent writers and allowed for a kind of ridicule of her appearance that diminished respect for her achievements as a writer and scholar.

Many subsequent studies took their cue from Shaw and the most venomous account of the family came in 1952 from the Belfast playwright St John Ervine, a biographer of Shaw, who

---

11. Frank Harris, *Oscar Wilde* (New York: Dorset Press, 1989), p. 330.
12. Ibid., p. 331.
13. Ibid., p. 334.
14. See George Bernard Shaw, *The Playwright and the Pirate,* ed. Stanley Weintraub (Gerrard's Cross: Colin Smythe, 1982), p. 33.

asserts that 'Neither of the Wildes had any sanctity to dispense.' The cruelty of his approach can be seen in this casual aside: 'Their second son Oscar was damned on the day that he was born and would have done better to have died in childhood as his sister Isola, who followed him, did.'[15]

In this study, I will demonstrate Jane Wilde's intellectual acuity and the diversity of her intellectual concerns. For another biographer, Horace Wyndham, that very range was, bizarrely, a sign of her frivolity: 'The trouble with Lady Wilde was that where her output was concerned, she wandered (and often floundered) in too many fields.'[16] Having maligned the diversity of her interests, Wyndham goes on to undermine her seriousness about her writing, 'Unfortunately, she professed to value intellectual culture not only above all else, but as the only object in life; and this grave mistake brought upon her tragic consequences.'[17] Again, her scholarship is made a weakness rather than a strength.

I argue in my study, *Oscar's Shadow,* that cultural and social changes remade Ireland's view of Oscar Wilde in the late twentieth century and into the twenty-first. Firstly, his Irishness and then his sexuality were reclaimed and made part of mainstream Irish identity as Ireland remade laws around sexuality and around the autonomy of the body. I would argue that this process of re-assimilation into what we see as acceptably 'Irish' is now true for Jane Wilde and for her literary reputation. However, this process of reconsideration has been slower, more complex in her case and, in many ways, more delayed. This is partly to do, I would argue, with a reluctance to acknowledge the role of earlier nineteenth-century women writers within Irish cultural nationalism.

Recent scholarship has challenged this reluctance and

---

15. St John Ervine, *Oscar Wilde: A Present Time Appraisal* (New York: Morrow, 1952), p. 35.
16. Horace Wyndham, *Speranza: A Biography of Lady Wilde* (London: Boardman, 1952), p. 162.
17. Ibid., p. 162.

successfully identified the broader role of Irish women within the discourse of Irish republicanism and not just during the Celtic Revival. New critical approaches to class, gender and national identity revitalises our view of her importance. In the words of Clíona Ó'Gallchoir and Heather Ingman in their introduction to the recent *A History of Modern Irish Women's Literature*, 'The project of writing a history of modern Irish women's literature at this moment in time has however been enabled not only by the achievements of scholars working on women's writing and feminist criticism but also by a marked shift within Irish literary historiography more generally.'[18] This study of Jane Wilde is part of a current reclamation of neglected Irish women writers of the nineteenth and twentieth century and their context within European intellectual culture. For me, my earlier research on the Irishness of Oscar Wilde brought me into contact with the considerable range of Jane Wilde's scholarship and her writings. From then, my interest was in reclaiming this fascinating corpus of lost poetry and prose. I produced a selection of her essays and writings, along with those of William Wilde and she was also a key figure in my novel, *The Diary of Mary Travers*.

Thus, contemporary thinking on Jane Wilde has changed in the twenty-first century and much for the better, particularly in the work of Wilde scholars like Eleanor Fitzsimons and Karen Tipper. In *The Fall of the House of Wilde*, Emer O'Sullivan argues: 'In many biographies of Oscar Wilde, Jane and William are not given their due. This does not square with the eminence Jane and William enjoyed in Ireland. Neither does it fit in with Oscar's view of them.'[19] Much of my thinking is influenced by these excellent studies and by my own research on the selected writings of Jane and William Wilde.

Renewed scholarly interest on the Wildes has included

---

18. Clíona Ó'Gallchoir and Heather Ingman, p. 4.
19. Emer O'Sullivan. *The Fall of the House of Wilde* (London: Bloomsbury, 2016), p. x.

conferences at Trinity College Dublin and The Royal College of Surgeons, Dublin, and the Royal Irish Academy. Studies like *The Fall of the House of Wilde, The Wilde Legacy,* and the recent publication of several volumes of Jane's letters and a critical study by Karen Tipper have all contributed to this reassessment. Indeed, Karen Tipper has been a valuable source of scholarship in the revival of Jane's academic reputation, with several edited volumes of her letters now available in print. While her 2002 study is not a literary biography but provides an ideal introduction to her writings as a nationalist, poet, teacher, and translator.[20]

Another important voice in the revaluation of Jane Wilde is that of the Irish novelist and critic, Colm Tóibín. He remarks on Wilde's respect for his mother in his 2002 essay, a prescient work that anticipates much of revisionism on Jane Wilde: 'In all of Oscar Wilde's letters which he refers to his mother, there is not one word of mockery or disloyalty. Mostly he refers to her not as his mother but as Lady Wilde.'[21] Colm Tóibín also makes the insightful point that all grotesque accounts of Jane only surface after Wilde's trials and disgrace: 'Before 1895 all the contemporary accounts of her are respectful and admiring of her scholarship and her literary standing.'[22]

In this book, I structure my study of Jane Wilde in in the following way and consider the range of her writings within the context of her life. In the first two sections, I look at her education, her career as the poet Speranza, and the crucial importance of her poems for *The Nation* in the revolutionary years of the late 1840s. I consider the vital importance of translation for her aesthetic and her knowledge of French and German literature in their making of her imagination. In the third section, I look at

---

20. Karen Tipper, *A Critical Biography of Jane Wilde* (New York: Edwin Millen, 2013), p. 3.
21. Colm Tóibín, *Love in a Dark Time: Gay Lives from Wilde to Almodóvar* (London: Picador 2002), p. 46.
22. Ibid., p. 51.

her life in Merrion Square, her translations and poems, and the ways in which her salon contributed to Irish cultural life. Finally, after William Wilde's death, Jane Wilde's move to London and her founding of a lively salon for younger writers there will be my focus. I will be detailing her London essays, her poetry and her travel writing, her nationalism, and her attitude towards culture, marriage and education.

Finally, in the year of her bicentenary, 2021, Ireland continued the process of reclaiming Jane Wilde as poet, translator, essayist, and critic. On International Women's Day in March 2021, the Irish postal authority issued a stamp in her honour. In December, Merlin Holland, her great-grandson, participated in a celebration of her scholarship with Noreen Doody in the Royal Irish Academy, called 'Speranza, A Scholar Reclaimed.' Crucially in November 2021, the Lord Mayor of Dublin unveiled a plaque at Number One, Merrion Square in her honour, where the achievements of her son Oscar and her husband William had already been celebrated with plaques for several years. This long-overdue ceremony was a fitting tribute to the importance of place in her career and a recognition that her status as an Irish woman writer had been overlooked.

Jane Wilde is worth remembering for the scope of her scholarly ambitions, her place within cultural politics and her contribution to Irish culture. Overall, my intention is to provide an account of the life and the achievements of Jane Wilde and to provide a full bibliography of current critical research so that the contemporary young Irish writers who gathered in One, Merrion Square to revive her salon in November 2019 will have a full account of their predecessor and understand her relevance for contemporary Irish writing and culture.

CHAPTER ONE

Education (1821–1845)

Strong nations fight, oppressed nations sing; and thus, not with armies and fleets, but with the passionate storm of lyric words have the Irish people kept up for centuries their ceaseless war against alien rule.[1]

Jane Frances Elgee was born into a prosperous, middle-class Protestant family in Dublin on 27th December 1821. It was one of her poetic fancies to suggest that Elgee was originally an Italian name, derived from Alighieri and thus linking her to Dante Alighieri. The reality was that her father, Charles Elgee, was a son of John Elgee, Archbishop of Wexford, and the Elgee family had come to Ireland from County Durham in England in the 1730s, to make money in the building trade. The family had prospered over the years and, by the time she was born, had made connections by marriage with many important Irish Protestant families.

Archdeacon John Elgee's eldest son, Charles, was Jane Wilde's father. Charles Elgee was a solicitor and in 1809, married her mother Sarah Kingsbury, the daughter of another clergyman, from a well-connected Dublin family with several literary connections. Sarah Kingsbury's grandfather, Dr Thomas Kingsbury, was President of the Royal College of Physicians and had been a close friend of Jonathan Swift. (It's not clear if Jane Wilde knew of this link with Swift as she failed to mention it in her essay on Stella and

---

1. Jane Wilde, 'Thomas Moore' in Eibhear Walshe, *Selected Writings of Speranza and William Wilde*, p. 196.

Vanessa, the two central women in Swift's life.) Sarah Kingsbury's sister Henrietta was married to the Irish novelist and playwright Charles Maturin, author of the 1820 novel, *Melmoth the Wanderer*. Maturin, unlike the rest of her family, had denounced the Act of Union of 1800. Later, in exile, her son Oscar would use the name Sebastian Melmoth, when trying to hide his criminalised identity in France and Italy.

Jane Elgee was brought up in the centre of Dublin, at 34 Leeson Street, and had a much older sister Emily, born 1811, and a brother John born in 1812. It seems as if the Elgee family experienced financial difficulties and the marriage of her parents had uneasy moments. As a result, her father died in India in 1825, where he had gone to repair the family fortunes. Thus, Jane Wilde was brought up by her mother and her education was, as I surmise, conducted at home. Later in life, she had few connections with her brother and sister and it is not unlikely that they disapproved of her politics and her fame. Her brother made a great deal of money but left her nothing in his will and her sister was living in England when Jane Wilde moved to London after the death of her husband, William, but there is no evidence of any contact between them.

As a young woman, mainly self-taught, with the assistance of tutors, Jane Wilde acquired several European languages, allowing her to develop a broad intellectual grounding for the impressive range of writings she was to produce. Her writings show her to have been familiar with the works of Kant and many other writers of the German Enlightenment. In addition, her writings show her love for Dante, Cervantes and Calderón and reflect her knowledge of Scandinavian poetry and myth. How she gained this impressive education is something of a mystery, as is the case with so many women writers in the nineteenth and early twentieth century. However, as this study will show, she possessed confidence and fluency with European languages, as her rich corpus of translations and essays demonstrates. There is some little biographical information available as to her education, her influences, and her formation as a writer. One biographer, Terence De Vere White suggests that her uncle, Richard Elgee, a classical scholar, may have been one of her educators[2] and she clearly had both Latin and Greek. What is known is that, by her mid-twenties, she was at the forefront of Irish writing as a poet and translator. This range and diversity as a poet allowed her to become an emblematic national figure in the resistance to British Rule in Ireland in the mid-nineteenth century and to draw on European ideas of nationalism and of revolution which were available to her via her talent for languages. It even led her to be viewed as dangerous by the British authorities in Dublin because of the treasonous and seditious nature of her poetry, and, as we will see, almost landed her in jail. She seemed to have acquired that European perspective without the kind of travel opportunities that many other writers had. Apart from a short trip to Scotland before she married, there is no evidence that she travelled in Europe. In addition to her keen interest in other languages and her proficiency as a translator, she was widely read in many fields; philosophy, drama, literature, folk traditions and ethnology, and politics. This variety of intellectual interests directly informed her essays. Her knowledge of French and German was such that she was to translate widely from both languages, and her translations would later stand as popular editions for many other writers and visual artists and still attract praise for her fluency and accessibility.

Her dedication to her writing is evident in this 1850 letter to her Scottish friend, John Hilson, where she describes her working day.[3] Jane Wilde met Hilson (1821–1884), a tweed manufacturer, of Lady's Yards, Jedburgh, while she was on holiday in Scotland with cousins in August 1847. A twenty-year correspondence ensued, although they never met again. They shared literary and

---

2. De Vere White, p. 85.
3. See Jean Muir, 'Speranza And Gurth: Jane Francesca Elgee's "unknown Scottish friend".' *The Wildean,* No. 21 (July 2002), pp. 2–14.

political interests and a keen admiration for the writings of Thomas Carlyle. Hilson married three times and, like Jane Wilde, was to suffer the loss of his children and she wrote to him to console and to reflect on loss and on death. Jean Muir makes the point that 'None of John Hilson's letters is known to have survived, but in her letters Jane thanks him for sending her copies of articles he has written – 'all the late manifestations of your rich and glowing spirit.'[4] These letters provide a useful insight into her working life living at home and not yet married, and her ideas and influences.

Jane Wilde was a disciplined and hard-working writer and she describes her daily routine to Hilson in this letter:

> I rise at ten or often eleven, glide down to breakfast which Mamma has all arranged for me. Breakfast over, I plunge into my ink bottle. Silence and solitude reign in the drawing room until two o'clock, for everyone knows I admit no visitor before that hour. We dine between five and six, after which I have the whole evening to myself. Mamma takes a siesta till tea at eight o'clock. I read and write in my room, descend to tea, the eternal pen or book until eleven o'clock, when Mamma departs to rest – I to my room where the midnight lamp is seen burning by observant neighbours until three.[5]

This lifelong habit of dedicated study and writing was the key to her great productivity and versatility as a scholar, poet and essayist.

By her own account, she was an autodidact. In later life, in an essay for the journal *Hearth and Home* in June 1892, she wrote, 'My favourite study was languages. I succeeded in mastering ten of the European languages. Till my eighteenth year I never wrote anything. All my time was given to study.'[6] (The one flaw of her education, self-confessed, was her untidy handwriting). Her

---

4. Muir, p. 5.
5. Eleanor Fitzsimons, *Wilde's Women* (London: Duckworth, 2015), p. 28.
6. Melville, p. 8.

enthusiasm for European literature was key to the achievements of her writings, in particular her poetry, where she found models and forms in French and German poetry to express her anger and her sorrow at the harrowing conditions of her country, especially during the Great Famine of 1845–8. Her interest in German and French poetry allowed her to establish her own unique poetic idiom and become the voice of her generation, via *The Nation*, a nationalist journal. (There is no evidence that she acquired Irish and all of her folklore collecting was without the help of direct knowledge of the Irish language, and came later in her career, in her time in London in the 1880s.)

For the young Jane Wilde, poetry was a key force for the implementation of political change. Her assessment of the career of her predecessor, Thomas Moore, is revealing in that it touches on the central tenet of her own creative principles. Her own poetic credo was that rebellion could be achieved by the compelling power of the imagination, 'passionate storms of lyric words', particularly when confronting overwhelming military and economic force. Education was also key in the work of the poet. For Jane Wilde, it was the specific vocation of the Irish nationalist poet to re-educate the Irish reading public, remedy the wilful neglect of successive British administrations and reawaken the dormant and neglected spirit of the Celtic imagination. Thomas Moore was one of several exemplars in her path to find her voice as an Irish nationalist poet and she paid tribute to him in the essay quoted above. Thomas Carlyle (1795–1881) was another influence and she was particularly taken with Carlyle's notion of a government of heroes, something that would illuminate her poetry of dissent and of nationalist fervour. A recent biographer, Emer O'Sullivan, has noted the influence of Carlyle's 'belief that dilettantism was almost a mortal sin and that the supreme justification of man's life was honest work solidly performed.'[7] This belief in the role

---

7. O'Sullivan, p. 49.

of solid work for the writer gave Jane Wilde a clear sense of her own vocation. O'Sullivan suggests that the young Jane Wilde 'echoed Carlyle's counsel when she wrote in one of her essays, 'Be earnest, earnest, earnest; mad if thou wilt; do what thou dost as if the stake were heaven.'[8] She was not always in agreement with Carlyle, disliking his life of Cromwell, but her sense that literature was the modern church and a way to unite all sectarian difference came from her reading of his works. Her life-long interest in his writings led to her reviewing some of his works in her later career in London and once, Carlyle sent her a copy of Tennyson's poems.

The decision to become a writer was facilitated by the fact that Jane Wilde lived at a time when there was a lively and successful publishing culture for Irish women. Anne Colman reckons that 'This was a fertile period for Irish women who were actively publishing for an eager audience. Between 1800 and 1900, more than five hundred women were writing and publishing throughout all genres.'[9] As Anne Colman suggests, 'Translation was a common writing activity for nineteenth-century women, particularly during the latter part of the century. A variety of languages were translated, with several women notably proficient in multiple languages.'[10] Jane Wilde was always good at identifying what would be of most interest to a reading public and to editors and publishers and was willing to try new forms and genres. Translation was key for her creativity and when she came to edit a collection of her poems *Poems by Speranza,* she created a section called 'Wanderings through European Literature,' marking the difference between her own original poems and her translations. Whether Jane Wilde had Russian, for example, is not clear. We

---

8. Ibid., p 50.
9. Anne Colman, 'Far from Silent: Nineteenth-Century Irish Women Writers' in *Gender Perspectives in Nineteenth-Century Ireland: Public and Private Spheres, Society for the Study of Nineteenth Century Ireland, 2,* ed. by Margaret Kelleher and James H. Murphy (Dublin: Irish Academic Press, 1997), p. 203.
10. Colman, p. 206.

know from her letters that she had difficulties in getting Russian dictionaries and so had little access to a means of learning Russian but she included a Russian poem in the translation section of her collected works.

Thematically she was drawn to writings where poets expressed rage against imperial oppression or professed an uncompromising love for one's own country. For example, in 'Le Reveille', published in *The Nation* in April 1846, she celebrates a place where 'Liberty's torch is bright', a translation from the poem by Georg Herwegh (1817–1875), a poet of the Young Germany movement. Direct political action is called for in this poem. The young man must leave his lover and blood must flow like a torrent to ensure the liberty of his people and his country. She published another translation of Herwegh's 'The Knight's Pledge' in May 1846 and here those young men who prepare for a bloody death do so for their country's freedom. Her version was published in *The Nation* on 16th May 1846:

> Our loved ones! Ah, the glass is clear.
> The cannon thunders, grasp the spear,
> We'll pledge them in a sigh.
> Now, on the foe like thunder crash!
> We'll scathe them like a lightening-flash,
> And conquer, though we die.

There is a connection between her aesthetic attraction towards European nationalist poetry and her nationalist politics. Her allegiance to the cause of Irish cultural nationalism was very much her own, dissenting from her family's unionist beliefs. She drew on her education and her knowledge of European political thought to critique the beliefs of her own class and her own family and this led to estrangement between her and her family. In her movement away from the more usual beliefs of her class, Jane Wilde was aware of a potential accusation of political and cultural appropriation.

She later recounted this anecdote about her Wexford grandfather and the rebellion of 1798 in her book, *Ancient Cures, Charms and Usages of Ireland*. It was her way of establishing a family tradition of sympathy and affinity with their Catholic neighbours who were part of the rebellion, and who threatened the Church of Ireland parishioners of her Elgee grandfather.

> On the day the rebels entered Wexford, the rector, Archdeacon Elgee assembled a few of the parishioners in the church to partake of the sacrament together, knowing that a dreadful death awaited them. On his return, the rebels were already forcing their way into his house; they seized him and the pikes were already at his breast when a man stepped forward and told of some great act of kindness which the Archdeacon had shown to his family. In an instant, the feeling changed and the leader gave orders that the archdeacon and all that belonged to him should be held safe from harm.[11]

With this lineage, Jane Wilde prepared herself to write for Ireland.

---

11. Wilde, Jane, *Ancient Cures, Charms and Usages of Ireland* (London: Ward & Downey, 1890), p. 228.

CHAPTER TWO

Inventing Speranza (1845–1851)

With all these resources, Jane Wilde became a national figure of protest and dissent at a young age through her poetry and her journalism. The magnitude of her achievements is worth noting. Although many of her own Church of Ireland background, including her own family, had supported the 1800 Act of Union, which abolished the Irish parliament in Dublin and moved direct rule to London, Jane Wilde herself became a committed republican. The years since the Act of Union had seen a sharp economic decline for Ireland, leading to greater social unrest and a consequent worsening of relations between the two countries. Irish political leaders had sought to redress the imbalance of representation for the Catholic majority by agitating for parliamentary reform, demanding greater political autonomy for Ireland and improved social and economic roles for the Catholic middle and working classes still impacted by discrimination on the grounds of religious background. One politician, Daniel O'Connell (1775–1847) emerged as an inspirational leader for this nationalist movement. O'Connell, known as the Great Liberator, was a politician, writer and lawyer, and he founded the Catholic Association in 1823, to campaign for representation for the Irish Catholic middle class. He succeeded in getting a Catholic Emancipation bill passed in Westminster in 1829. This meant that Catholic men of property and influence could, for the first time, be elected to parliament and could therefore agitate directly on the reform of Irish governance. The result was an Irish party in parliament in Westminster from 1830 onwards, a grouping that could lobby for greater Irish political self-determination right at the centre of imperial power and legislation. In 1830, O'Connell became the first Catholic MP to take his seat at Westminster and from there, he led the Irish MPs, a defining figure in the struggle for Irish political autonomy.

By the time Jane Wilde was publishing her poems in the mid-1840s, much of the excitement of these earlier political achievements had been dissipated. Instead, Ireland in the 1840s was a place of discontent and seething revolution, as was much of Europe. She wrote to attack the inequalities of British rule, specifically the disastrous ineptitude of the Westminster government's handling of the crisis of the Great Famine and she called for active rebellion. She found herself allied with many other young Irish activists, journalists and political dissenters from all classes and all professions, and they found common cause and solidarity with the wider European movement of unrest and revolution in the mid-1840s.

Younger writers and activists like Jane Wilde were unhappy with the continued political stalemate in Ireland. To them, O'Connell was a leader now past his prime and his usefulness. He, in turn, distrusted them and believed them to be anti-clerical. Like many of her generation, she drew on contemporary European literary influences for her own, distinct poetic voice and to create poems that would incite revolt and undermine the political establishment. For Jane Wilde, as for many of her generation, Byron was a crucial influence as a poet actively engaged in war and rebellion. She was in accord with her literary hero in regarding politics and poetry as possessing an urgent and necessary interconnection. As already mentioned, Byron's friend, the writer and lyricist Thomas Moore (1779–1852) provided Jane Wilde with another, more direct influence. Moore influenced her not only in form, both using the popular poetic form of the ballad, but also by drawing both national and international attention to the woes and inequalities of his beleaguered country. Later, during her time in London, she published a lengthy essay on Moore where she celebrated the undoubted fact that, 'Through Moore's lyrics, set to the pathetic Irish music, the wrongs of Ireland were first made known to Europe, and the sympathy excited by them for a people so gifted and so unfortunate materially helped to break the terrible and insulting bondage of the penal laws.'[1] For her, this linking of creativity with political protest was powerful, and her essay on Moore tells us a great deal about her own concept of the relationship between poet and country. As someone who came from an Irish Protestant heritage, Jane Wilde is, nevertheless, keenly aware of the subordinate position and the humiliations suffered by an educated Catholic like Moore and comments 'What wonder if he felt bitterly and expressed openly his detestation of English rule?'[2]

What most inspired Jane Wilde about Moore was the way in which he drew on Irish themes, music and sources to create his *Melodies*. She admired the way in which they became international, transcending all sectarian identities and making their creator celebrated as a poet of liberty and freedom:

> The magic influence that at last unsealed the fount and revealed to the poet the riches of his genius, came from the divinely beautiful spirit of Irish music. At once, when it touched his soul, the hidden stream of inspiration rushed up to heaven, clear and pure and sparkling, and fell to earth again in showers of many coloured splendours, strengthening and refreshing not only his own loved land, but stimulating amongst the far-off nations the growth of Freedom's goodly tree.[3]

---
1. Walshe, *Selected Writings of Speranza* pp. 195–196.
2. Ibid., p. 196.
3. Ibid., p. 198.

This was to be her own ambition, to draw on Irish sources and themes, to promote liberty and the struggle for political freedom and then for her poems to resonate in foreign cultures. To some degree, this was what she achieved, and in a very short space of time.

Becoming a public figure in the world of nationalist protest was not only going against the unionist beliefs of her own class but was also flouting the constraints placed on women in public life in Victorian society. To be well known, for a woman, risked being regarded as morally suspect. At first, as we will see, she used a male pen name, to protect her identity but soon, with the name Speranza, Jane Wilde was prepared to take that risk and become notorious, if her true identity were ever discovered. Later she was to write of this period of Irish history, 'A delirium of patriotic excitement raged through the land as these young orators and poets flashed the full light of their genius on the wrongs, the hopes, and the old heroic memories of their country; even the upper classes in Ireland awoke for the first time to the sense of the nobleness of a life devoted to national regeneration.'[4] To be visible as a young woman within such a revolutionary generation required a greater commitment of patriotic excitement and she was prepared for that commitment. After her death, this visibility was used against her, to the detriment of her reputation as a writer and a scholar.

Her belief in the cause of Irish freedom had the depth of a religious faith and remained unwavering. In later life, to explain why she was converted to the cause of Irish nationalism, she dramatised one single moment of youthful epiphany. In what was clearly a moment of dramatic invention, she told Yeats that when she was a young woman: 'Walking through some Dublin street, she came upon so great a crowd that she could go no further,' Yeats recalled her telling him. 'She asked a shop man what brought so many people into the street, and he said, "It is the funeral of

---

4. Ibid., p. 167.

Thomas Davis", and when she answered, "Who is Thomas Davis, I have never heard of him?" He said, "He was a poet."[5]

Jane Wilde grew up on Leeson Street, right in the centre of Dublin, near Merrion Square, and would have been aware of all the important political events happening around her in the capital. Yet she saw herself as politically uninformed until she began to read the poetry and the prose of contemporaries like Davis. Thomas Davis, a Protestant barrister and poet, was a national figure by the time of his early death in 1845 at the age of thirty-one. Of course, she would have known who Thomas Davis was. His death was a moment of national mourning. Yet, she needed to construct her conversion to the cause of Irish nationalism as a moment of sudden revelation, a decisive turning away from the political beliefs of her own class and her family in a blinding flash of recognition. Dissent was key to Jane Wilde's sense of her own aesthetic and she sought to dramatise that process of political self-education into one cathartic experience. However much she dramatised or invented this moment, it should be said that this was to be no temporary moment of conversion. Her life work as a poet, essayist and collector of Irish folklore was all inspired and motivated by this moment of realisation. She was unwavering in her commitment to the revival and preservation of Irish literature as a cultural parallel to the struggle for Irish political autonomy. Revolution prompted her first poems.

The Nation was the journal in which Jane Wilde made her reputation. This journal had been set up by Thomas Davis with the young writers and activists Charles Gavan Duffy (1816–1903) and John Blake Dillon (1814–1866) in October 1842 and soon became a popular forum for the younger generation. These young men, frustrated at the political stagnation of their country and impatient at what they saw as the failures of Daniel O'Connell to achieve further reform in London, pushed for more radical action.

---

5. Melville, p. 20.

The Nation soon became a focus for Irish writers, who wanted to promote a more engaged sense of nationhood across the divided classes and religious groups. They were soon known as the Young Irelanders because of similarities between their aims and those of Heinrich Heine and the Young Germany movement of the 1830s and the Young Italy movement led by Giuseppe Mazzini. The motto of the young Irelanders was 'Educate that You May Be Free.'

Charles Gavan Duffy, a Catholic journalist from County Monaghan, was, at this point, an experienced writer, and so he was appointed editor. Duffy was greatly influenced by the writings of Thomas Carlyle and had even accompanied him on his walking tour of Ireland in 1849. Jane Wilde was also widely read in Carlyle's work and in the works of many of the same German, French and Italian political thinkers. Duffy had been imprisoned in 1843 with Daniel O'Connell and was a key figure in the agitation to undo the Act of Union between England and Ireland and restore some form of home rule or autonomy to Ireland. The demands for reform were becoming increasingly urgent amongst the younger political activists. O'Connell, uneasy as to their motives, was not sympathetic to the methods of the 'Young Irelanders.' Nor were they sympathetic to him or to his legacy. Duffy was prominent within this faction. Jane Wilde became part of their world, writing to a friend that, 'There is an earnestness almost amounting to fanaticism in the Patriotism of all of the young Ireland party combined with great genius and a glowing poetical transcendentalism. They are all poets and I know of no genius outside their circle in Ireland.'[6]

Although she never writes of the others, Jane Wilde was one of several young women writing for *The Nation*. These included 'Eva', the pseudonym of Mary Anne Kelly (later O'Doherty) (1825–1910). 'Eva' also came from a staunch unionist background, also translated Lamartine and would eventually go on to translate other French works, in her case, principally the poetry of Pierre-

---

6. O'Sullivan, p. 50.

Jean de Béranger. These women were not remembered, and as Anne Coleman writes, 'A thorough study of women writers associated with *The Nation* has yet to be undertaken. Although Mary Anne Kelly O'Doherty ('Eva'), Ellen Mary Patrick Downing ('Kate', 'Ellen' and 'Mary') and Lady Jane Francesca Elgee Wilde ('Speranza') are frequently cited, lesser-known women remain unexplored: Kate Cuihane, Fanny Forrester, Olivia Knight, Katharine Mary Murphy, Ellen O'Leary, Marie M. Thompson, Jane Verner, Elizabeth Willoughby Treacy Varian, to name but a few.'[7] Later the writings of 'Eva', Mary Anne Kelly O'Doherty will be discussed.

Jane Wilde began contributing to *The Nation* in February 1846, with a translation of a German poem called 'The Holy War.' She chose the pen name Speranza to imbue her poems with that sense of hope and excitement that was paramount for young people in this decade of revolution and thus aligning herself to the radical traditions of her contemporaries within European literature. The 1840s were clearly a time of great excitement and fulfilment for her and she told a correspondent in December 1848 that, 'I should like to rage through life this orthodox creeping is too tame for me – ah, this wild rebellious nature of mine. I wish I could satiate it with Empires though a St. Helena were the end.'[8] The allusion to Napoleon was not accidental. Her knowledge of French literature and society shaped her vision of what Irish revolutionary society meant for her as an Irish woman. She was later to write of the role of Irish women in political life in sharp, depreciating terms, suggesting a parallel with French society that was to Ireland's distinct disadvantage: 'While reading of Lamartine's brilliant descriptions of the women who led French society at that period, one cannot help animadvertising, par parentheses [sic], on the absurd idea prevalent amongst us, that politics should not be discussed by a woman – as if the destiny of her country was not

---

7. Colman, p. 205.
8. Melville, p. 53.

a nobler object for thought and subject for conversation than the gossip of a neighbourhood. French ladies are wiser.'[9] Irish women were central to revolution in the nineteenth and early twentieth century, women like Kathleen Lynn, (1874–1955) Constance Markievicz, (1868–1927) Maud Gonne (1866–1953) and many others. Jane Wilde's example was important in terms of challenging any patriarchal limitations and constraints for successive generations.

When she began to submit her poems, Charles Gavan Duffy had not yet met the author in person. Her first publication came in February 1846, with a translation of a German poem, 'The Holy War', where a new leader is wished for, someone who inspires a generation and make a radical change to the nature of a stagnant society. This poem was accompanied by a letter written by Jane Wilde using the pseudonym John Fanshaw Ellis, a male name, with her initials Jane Francesca Elgee. Many Victorian women writers used male pen names, to protect themselves from prurient and unwelcome publicity as to the 'unnaturalness' of a woman holding a prominent public position. As it happened, Jane Wilde was to prove that very point, subject to intense misogynistic ridicule after her death. She may have thought that a male poet would initially be taken more seriously, and she knew that her family would disapprove. In the event, they did find out about her secret authorship of seditious poems and one uncle reproved her, declaring the journal was only fit for the fire. It is not recorded if this was her uncle Richard, who may have taught her Latin and Greek, arming her with the learning to subvert the dearly-held unionist political beliefs of her family, but it was likely.[10]

Jane Wilde was published by Duffy who was curious to meet 'him' and even put a request in the 'Answers to Correspondents' section calling on 'Mr. Ellis' to make himself known. Finally, she

---

9. Jane Wilde, *Notes on Men, Women and Books* (London: Ward & Downey, 1891), p. 104.
10. Melville, p. 18.

agreed, and they met. These are Duffy's recollections of the first meeting:

> I was greatly struck by the first contribution and requested Mr. John Fanshawe Ellis to call at the *Nation* office. A smiling parlour maid when I inquired for Mr. Ellis showed me into a drawing room.... a tall girl whose stately carriage and figure, flashing brown eyes and features cast in a heroic mould, seemed fit for the genius of poetry or the spirit of revolution.[11]

They became friends, with many political views in common, and Jane Wilde came to admire him greatly, calling him, 'A man of the highest culture, of exquisite literary taste and a clear and powerful writer, both in prose and verse, he was eminently fitted for guide and counsellor to all the young fiery intellects that composed his staff, while his winning manners and earnest sympathy with all that was noble and beautiful in literature and art gained their admiration and love.'[12]

Her time with *The Nation* was a fruitful one in that she found her own original voice as a poet partly through the translations that allowed her to comment on the current Irish political crisis via European literature. Michael Cronin has written that, 'The bulk of Speranza's translated verse was published in *The Nation* newspaper in 1846. The source languages for her translations were French, German, Italian, Spanish, Portuguese and Russian. German was the dominant source language and between 1846 and 1848 she produced seventeen separate translations from German.'[13] This interest in translation radicalised her own writings and gave her the aesthetic foregrounding to become a national figure.

From 1846 until 1848, her most directly political poems

---

11. Gavan Duffy, *My Life in Two Hemispheres* (Dublin: Unwin, 1898) p. 75.
12. Jane Wilde, *Ancient Cures,* p. 178.
13. Michael Cronin, 'Lady Jane "Speranza" Wilde and the Translator's Invisibility,' *Claritas* 8 (2002), p. 8.

like 'The Stricken Land', 'The Fall of the Tyrants', and 'The Year of Revolutions,' were all published in *The Nation*. These poems directly supported the political work of her fellow Young Irelanders and found a wide and appreciative audience. In 'The Young Patriot Leader,' published in October 1846, she eulogised her fellow revolutionary Thomas Francis Meagher (1823–1867) in these terms:

> Oh, he stands beneath the sun, that Glorious Fated One
> Like a martyr or conqueror, wearing
> On his brow a mighty doom, be it glory, be it gloom,
> The shadow of a crown it is bearing.

Meagher, dubbed 'Meagher of the Sword' for his eloquence, had been denounced by O'Connell as a secret enemy of the Catholic Church. In contrast, Jane Wilde was an admirer of Meagher and supported him when he was arrested for sedition in August 1848. His speech from the dock when he was sentenced to death was one of a series of celebrated political speeches made during the nineteenth century by Irish revolutionaries, eloquent in their defiance of British rule in Ireland.

Writing the Famine

> 'Poetry as popular song became an important weapon in the long war against colonialism. Since it was then widely assumed throughout Europe that the ballad was the original poetry of the people, nationalist movements tended to give it unprecedented political prominence. This prominence was buoyed by the wide distribution of political poems and ballads in popular nationalist newspapers.[14]

---

14. Seamus Deane, 'Poetry and Song 1800–1890' in *The Field Day Anthology of Irish Writing*, vol. 2, edited by Seamus Deane et al. (Derry: Field Day, 1991), pp. 1–9.

Jane Wilde came into being as a poet precisely at a moment of great distress and anxiety in her country. Her importance as a Famine poet partly rests on her ability to use her poems for imagined first-hand experiences of the trauma of starvation and death. Despite, and also because of her relatively privileged upbringing as a writer, she was determined to represent the immediate and disastrous consequences of the Famine for the working class in stark and dramatic poetic form. There is no evidence that Jane Wilde spent any time outside Dublin during the years of the Famine and so her writings may not have been based on her first-hand observations. Her future husband William Wilde, on the other hand, was working directly as a doctor in the West of Ireland all during this time and would write about his medical observations. Nevertheless, Jane Wilde's poetic voice was one of the most effective during this time at personalising the disaster of famine and one of the most empathetic.

Christopher Morash argues that the urgency to write about the Famine was primarily political: 'For these men and women, bearing witness to the scale of horror was both an ethical and a strategic necessity, narrating that which needed to be said and at the same time disrupting the discourse of what Mitchel so acidly calls 'British Civilisation'.[15] Morash sees James Clarence Mangan's poetry as realising a fully subversive potential, particularly in his 1848 poem, 'A Vision' and makes a comparison with Jane Wilde, pointing out that this Mangan poem 'opens with the foregrounding of the prophetic voice and the present-tense verb forms common to the poems of [...] Speranza and [her] anonymous counterparts':[16]

> In that spectralest hour,
> In that Valley of Gloom,

---

15. Christopher Morash, *Writing the Irish Famine* (Clarendon Press: Oxford, 1995), p. 102.
16. Morash, p. 120.

> Fell a Voice on mine ear,
> Like a wail from the tomb,
> Or that dread cry which Fear
> Gives our Angels of Doom,
> But of world-waking power.
> What it spake ye shall hear.[17]

This was the poetic culture in which she was writing and her work stood out for the passionate nature of her engagement and her gift for poetic storytelling. For Jane Wilde, poetry also had the potential for universal appeal and emotional connection and she shared with Mangan that gift for direct poetic utterance and prophecy. An entire country, regardless of class or religion, could be reached and moved and educated. In a much later essay called 'The Poet as Teacher', she wrote 'The poor in these rough northern climes have little time for the dreamy musings over the illuminated pages of Nature, to which the luxurious indolence of a southern existence gives such full facility. The sunset and the cloud, the spiritual influence of dying day, or of night with starry host; the grandeur of the lonely mountain, the song of waters, the choral music of the waving trees – all the beauty and melody of the world, is, in a great degree, mute and veiled to our weary toiling slaves of civilisation.'[18]

Her belief was that poetry could be populist, could transcend class, and unite across sectarian divides. Like many Irish writers in the later nineteenth century, like Synge and Augusta Gregory and W. B. Yeats, the need to find a universal voice for Irish poetry and folklore sprang from their own recognition that they came from a class associated with colonial rule in Ireland. As writers, they tried to accommodate themselves within the new Ireland and within the literary forms of Irish cultural nationalism

---

17. Sean Ryder, ed. *James Clarence Mangan: Selected Writings* (Dublin: UCD Press, 2004), p. 284.
18. Walshe, *Selected Writings of Speranza and William Wilde*, p. 232.

through their creativity. As Jane Wilde expressed it, 'literature, in the full plenitude of its ennobling influence, can reach all classes, the lowest as the highest. The words of man can permeate where the music of the forest trees never can be heard. In the cabin, the cellar, the factory, the mine, the children of the cities or the plains, wherever there is a soul however darkened, the souls of other men can reach him; the divine thinkers of all ages may come in and sit down by him, though his dwelling be the meanest hut.'[19] She needed to escape from the political legacy of her own class, beneficiaries of colonial rule, and find a role beyond sectarian identity.

When the blight struck in 1845, this was the first of three successive years when the potato crop failed. The potato was the staple diet for most of the small farmers of Ireland and their families, who found themselves in grave danger. This danger was compounded by the fact that, politically the *laissez-faire* trading policies adopted in Westminster increased economic hardship and suffering unnecessarily. This led to famine in one of the most fertile countries in the world. When the Famine reached its height in February 1847, a typhus epidemic also swept through the country and was responsible for the loss of many more lives. These non-interventionist policies adopted by the new Whig government in Westminster led to many deaths, over a million dead in a decade. Soup kitchens and relief works set up to help the starving population proved insufficient. Emigration was at a high and the Young Irelanders, initially for peaceful protest and non-sectarian strategies of resistance, now became increasingly militant and even violent in their rage at the inadequacies of the government's response to wholesale death. The country headed inexorably towards insurrection and Jane Wilde's writing became increasingly provocative as she sought to dramatise the plight of the betrayed and abandoned starving populace. Karen Tipper

---

19. Ibid., p. 229.

asserts that, 'In her poems on the Famine, Jane Wilde reveals her knowledge of the inhuman condition, her compassion for the widespread suffering, particularly that of the children and her anger at the social and political attitudes that she believed were responsible.'[20] Almost two centuries later, her poetry is widely regarded as a passionate and eloquent response to the catastrophe.

A key poem in this genre is 'The Stricken Land,' later republished 'The Famine Year' in January 1847, poetry creating the vivid impression of a first-hand witness account of the sufferings of the country people. As to whether Jane Wilde left Dublin and saw these scenes herself is not clear. In a sense, it doesn't matter. What was important was that she was using her imaginative power to envisage this world of suffering and death, for a reading audience and she is not afraid to accuse those responsible and to threaten eventual punishment from the Almighty. She is one of the few Irish poets to do so and to achieve a wide audience for her witness poetry. It is worth quoting this poem in full, as it was to prove one of her most popular and enduring work, later reproduced in such anthologies as Charles Read's *Cabinet of Irish Literature* in 1880 and then in the school text book, *Ballads of Irish History* in 1929. It opens with a question as to whether the Famine is a punishment for some earlier sin:

> Weary men, what reap ye? – Golden corn for the stranger.
> What sow ye? – Human corpses that wait for the avenger.
> Fainting forms, hunger-stricken, what see you in the offing?
> Stately ships to bear our food away, amid the stranger's scoffing.
> There's a proud array of soldiers – what do they need round your door?
> They guard our masters' granaries from the thin hands of the poor.

---

20. Tipper, p. 265.

Pale mothers, wherefore weeping? – Would to God that we were dead –
Our children swoon before us, and we cannot give them bread.

II.
Little children, tears are strange upon your infant faces,
God meant you but to smile within your mother's soft embraces.
Oh! we know not what is smiling, and we know not what is dying;
But we're hungry, very hungry, and we cannot stop our crying.
And some of us grow cold and white – and we know not what it means;
But, as they lie beside us, we tremble in our dreams.
There's a gaunt crowd on the highway – are ye come to pray to man,
With hollow eyes that cannot weep, and for words your faces wan?

III.
No; the blood is dead within our veins – we care not now for life;
Let us die hid in the ditches, far from children and from wife;
We cannot stay and listen to their raving, famished cries –
Bread! Bread! Bread! and none to still their agonies.
We left our infants playing with their dead mother's hand:
We left our maidens maddened by the fever's scorching brand:
Better, maiden, thou were strangled in thy own dark-twisted tresses –
Better, infant, thou wert smothered in thy mother's first caresses.

IV.
We are fainting in our misery, but God will hear our groan;
Yet, if fellow-men desert us, will He hearken from His Throne?
Accursed are we in our own land, yet toil we still and toil;
But the stranger reaps our harvest – the alien owns our soil.
O Christ! how have we sinned, that on our native plains
We perish houseless, naked, starved, with branded brow, like Cain's?
Dying, dying, wearily, with a torture sure and slow –
Dying, as a dog would die, by the wayside as we go.

V.
One by one they're falling round us, their pale faces to the sky;
We've no strength left to dig them graves – there let them lie.
The wild bird, if he's stricken, is mourned by the others,
But we – we die in Christian land – we die amid our brothers,
In the land which God has given, like a wild beast in his cave,
Without a tear, a prayer, a shroud, a coffin, or a grave.
Ha! but think ye the contortions on each livid face ye see,
Will not be read on judgment-day by eyes of Deity?

VI.
We are wretches, famished, scorned, human tools to build your pride,
But God will yet take vengeance for the souls for whom Christ died.
Now is your hour of pleasure – bask ye in the world's caress;
But our whitening bones against ye will rise as witnesses,
From the cabins and the ditches, in the charred, uncoffin'd masses,
For the Angel of the Trumpet will know them as he passes.
A ghastly, spectral army, before the great God we'll stand,
And arraign ye as our murderers, the spoilers of our land.

This poem takes the voice of those starving and makes them central to the dramatic power of the poem itself. As we will see, some of her other poems now appear to be overladen with a kind of high Victorian rhetoric, but in these Famine poems, she pares her language back to provide as direct and as dramatic a voice as possible. The disaster of Famine drew from Jane Wilde a directness and an attractive bluntness of poetic diction shared by many of the writers of *The Nation*. Morash notes the 'powerful textual strategy of writing the Famine as an apocalypse taking place in the "now" of the reader'.[21]

This and other of the poems included in this chapter were written to be recited in public. They proved popular for recitation and for a call to Irish nationalists to rebel and overthrow the government that was mishandling the calamity of Famine. To see these poems as fashioned for public performance goes a long way in terms of understanding their effectiveness. What was also so radical and innovative was that Jane Wilde gave voices to those who had been betrayed by the politicians. Those voices of the oppressed are defiant, proud, refusing to be seen as passive or cowed by hunger and death. The link is made with righteous anger and eventual revolution and punishment for those responsible and her poetic language is direct, sharp, crisp and without mercy. In the words of Matthew Campbell, 'Her poems on the Famine not merely intrude, they are focussed on the experience with an effect which approached shock, drawing into verse images of horror garnered from newspaper sketches and journalistic reports.'[22] Eiléan Ni Chuilleanáin suggests that Jane Wilde is no match for Mangan in terms of her poetic power but that the poems of *The Nation*, because they carry parables drawn from Irish history, have a narrative weight that brings more solidity

---

21 Morash, p. 112.
22. Matthew Campbell, "Poetry, 1845–90" in *A History of Modern Irish Women's Writing*, eds. Clíona Ó'Gallchoir and Heather Ingman (Cambridge: Cambridge University Press, 2018), p. 82.

and more endurance to her imagination:

> Within the Irish political canon of her century, she is a match perhaps for Thomas Davis but not for Allingham or Ferguson, certainly not for Mangan. Her language and her metre are quite different. They are energetic ... Speranza needs something to slow her down and in fact the most successful of her poems with their long lines and strong pauses have a drag on them, a drag of feeling as much as metre in "The Famine Year" and in the poem on Henry and John Sheares. Some of the extra weight that ballasts those two poems come from their sense of real history.[23]

The strength of her poem is echoed by such Famine poems as Mangan's 1849 poem 'The Funerals', written just before his death:

> What was this mystery? Years would seem
> To have rolled away,
> Before those Funerals halted on their path–
> Were they but mockeries of a dream?
> Or did the vision darkly say,
> That here were signs of looming wrath?
>
> I know not! But within the soul
> I know there lives
> A deep, a marvellous, a prophetic power,
> Far beyond even its own control –
> And why? Perchance because it gives
> Dread witness of a JUDGEMENT HOUR![24]

Jane Wilde's power as a poet is perhaps linked to her skills as a

---

23. Eiléan Ní Chuilleanáin, *The Wilde Legacy* (Dublin: Four Courts Press, 2003), p. 21.
24. Ryder, ed. *James Clarence Mangan*, p. 306.

storyteller in prose and therefore, another significant *Nation* poem, one of her most dramatic, works almost like a verse drama and concerns the fate of the Sheares brothers. John (1766–1798) and Henry Sheares (1753–1798) were two Corkmen who had studied the law, both qualifying as barristers. In 1792, they both spent time in Paris, during the French Revolution and became acquainted with leaders like Madame Roland and many others and came to believe in the necessity for armed rebellion. It was said that on the boat from France to England, they met with a young Daniel O'Connell and showed him a handkerchief soaked in the blood of Louis XVI that they treasured, a moment that revolted O'Connell and set him firmly against violent rebellion. The Sheares brothers returned to Dublin and Henry was elected president of the Society of United Irishmen. During the rebellion of 1798, they were both arrested and condemned to death. John made a plea for the life of his older brother but they were both hanged, drawn and quartered in July of 1798:

> I.
> 'TIS midnight, falls the lamp-light dull and sickly,
> On a pale and anxious crowd,
> Through the court, and round the judges, thronging thickly,
> With prayers none dare to speak aloud.
> Two youths, two noble youths, stand prisoners at the bar –
> You can see them through the gloom –
> In pride of life and manhood's beauty, there they are
> Awaiting their death doom.

The poem continues with a dramatisation of the nobility of their sacrifice and the veniality of those who had betrayed them and the poem is an interesting example of Jane Wilde's valorisation of Irish masculine honour and pride. This even-handedness of her representation of Irish working-class male identity is noted by Amy Martin: 'Elgee [Jane Wilde] uses a sophisticated exploration of gender and family to represent dehumanisation [...] At the same time, Elgee resists narratives of blame, or lapsing into stereotypes of Irish men as feminised, violent, or culturally deviant.'[25] Almost two centuries later, her poetry is highly regarded as a passionate and eloquent response to the catastrophe.

> Before them, shrinking, cowering, scarcely human,
> The base informer bends,
> Who, Judas-like, could sell the blood of true men,
> While he clasped their hands as friends.
> Aye, could fondle the young children of his victim,
> Break bread with his young wife,
> At the moment that for gold his perjured dictum
> Sold the husband and the father's life.
>
> V.
> There is silence in the midnight – eyes are keeping
> Troubled watch till forth the jury come;
> There is silence in the midnight – eyes are weeping –
> "Guilty!" – is the fatal uttered doom.
> For a moment o'er the brothers' noble faces
> Came a shadow sad to see;
> Then silently they rose up in their places,
> And embraced each other fervently.
>
> VI.
> Oh! the rudest heart might tremble at such sorrow,
> The rudest cheek might blanch at such a scene:
> Twice the judge essayed to speak the word – to-morrow –
> Twice faltered, as a woman he had been.

---

25. Amy Martin, 'The Skeleton at the Feast: Lady Wilde's Famine Poetry and Irish Internationalist Critiques of Food Scarcity,' in *Women and the Great Hunger*, eds. Christine Kinealy, Jason King, and Ciaran Reilly (Hamden, CT: Quinnipiac University Press, 2017), p. 151.

To-morrow! – Fain the elder would have spoken,
Prayed for respite, tho' it is not death he fears;
But thoughts of home and wife his heart hath broken,
And his words are stopped by tears.

VII.
But the youngest – oh, he spake out bold and clearly:–
"I have no ties of children or of wife;
Let me die – but spare the brother who more dearly
Is loved by me than life."
Pale martyrs, ye may cease, your days are numbered;
Next noon your sun of life goes down;
One day between the sentence and the scaffold –
One day between the torture and the crown!

VIII.
A hymn of joy is rising from creation;
Bright the azure of the glorious summer sky;
But human hearts weep sore in lamentation,
For the Brothers are led forth to die.
Aye, guard them with your cannon and your lances –
So of old came martyrs to the stake;
Aye, guard them – see the people's flashing glances,
For those noble two are dying for their sake.

IX.
Yet none spring forth their bonds to sever
Ah! methinks, had I been there,
I'd have dared a thousand deaths ere ever
The sword should touch their hair.
It falls! – there is a shriek of lamentation
From the weeping crowd around;
They're stilled – the noblest hearts within the nation –
The noblest heads lie bleeding on the ground.

X.
Years have passed since that fatal scene of dying,
Yet, lifelike to this day,
In their coffins still those severed heads are lying,
Kept by angels from decay.
Oh! they preach to us, those still and pallid features –
Those pale lips yet implore us, from their graves,
To strive for our birthright as God's creatures,
Or die, if we can but live as slaves.

This proved one of her most celebrated poems, widely reproduced and recited and heard on the streets of Dublin. Driving the poem is the idea of the nobility of the two Sheares brothers, the villainy of the men who had betrayed them to the government and the fact that the younger had pleaded for the life of the older. Men who die for each other, and who will sacrifice themselves for family are noble and true. This poem created resonances with the revolutionaries of 1848, where Thomas Francis Meagher and others of the Young Irelanders had been offered the death sentence or deportation to Australia and all had chosen to die martyrs' deaths.

The poem 'France in '93' drew on her lifelong interest in the parallels between Irish and French revolutionary society and her consistent preoccupation with situating Irish revolution with the upheavals of the French revolution as a warning to a complacent regime. As Emer O'Sullivan has commented, 'Undoubtedly this was meant to discomfit those responsible or complicit in the mismanagement of Famine.'[26]

Ye, the deaf ones to their cries –
Ye, who scorned their agonies –
'Tis no longer prayers for bread
Shriek in your ears the famished.

---

26. O'Sullivan, p. 44.

> But wildly, fiercely, peal on peal,
> Resoundeth – Down with the Bastille!
> Can ye tame a people now?
> Try them – flatter, promise, vow,
> Swear their wrongs shall be redressed –
> But patience – time will do the rest.
> Swear they shall one day be fed –
> Hark! the People – Dead for Dead!

This idea of a day of retribution, when the great masses of the Irish oppressed will be revenged on the hated British administration is also the theme of her political essays at this time:

> IV.
> Calculating statement, quail.
> Proud aristocrat, grow pale;
> Savage sounds that deathly song:
> Down with tyrants! Down with wrong!
> Blindly now they wreak revenge –
> How rudely do a mob avenge!
> What! coroneted Prince or Peer,
> Will not the base-born slavelings fear?
> Sooth, their cry is somewhat stern:
> Aristocrats, à la Lanterne!
> Ghastly fruit their lances bear –
> Noble heads with streaming hair;
> Diadem and kingly crown
> Strike the Famine-stricken down.
> Now, the People's work is done –
> On they stride o'er prostrate throne;
> Royal blood of King and Queen
> Streameth from the guillotine;
> Wildly on the people goeth,
> Reaping what the noble soweth.

> Little, dreamed he, prince or peer,
> Of who should be his heritor.
> Hunger now, at last, is sated
> In halls where once it wailed and waited;
> Wild Justice fiercely rives the laws
> Which failed to right a people's cause.
> On that human ocean floweth,
> Whither stops it no one knoweth –
> Surge the wild waves in their strength
> Against all chartered rights at length –
> Throne, and King, and Nobel fall;
> But the People – they hold Carnival!

Here, Jane Wilde achieves a chilling tone with the implicit threat of violence, the idea of an Irish people, no longer passive in the face of extinction or death, and the distinct possibility of a return to the dangerous anger that led to the execution of Louis XVI and Marie Antoinette. France is a warning example to the Irish establishment. As Morash comments, 'There were attempts to locate this dangerously transgressive moment in some sort of historical context.'[27]

Jane Wilde in her poem, 'The Year of the Revolutions' framed this Irish rebellion within the broader context of a time where all was in turmoil and monarchies and empires were under threat:

> Lift up your pale faces, ye children of sorrow,
> The night passes on to a glorious to-morrow!
> Hark! hear you not sounding glad Liberty's pæan,
> From the Alps to the Isles of the tideless Ægean?
> And the rhythmical march of the gathering nations,
> And the crashing of thrones 'neath their fierce exultations,
> And the cry of Humanity cleaving the ether,
> With hymns of the conquering rising together

---

27. Morash, p. 116.

God, Liberty, Truth! How they burn heart and brain
These words shall they burn—shall they waken in vain?

In another poem from this time, 'The Faithless Shepherds,' Jane Wilde directly attacks the Irish land-owning class, living off the rents, abdicating all responsibility for the lives and the survival of their tenants. Although she came from a more privilege social class than many Irish women and men at the time, she attacks the indolence and the negligence of those with property. For her, poetry always had a national and a political purpose. This sense of anger against the ruling class in Ireland was also to be a constant in her essays. In 'The Poet as Teacher,' a review of a book called *A Selection for Irish Children,* she argued that

> One of the many reasons, perhaps, of Ireland's degradation is, that her gentry were never taught to feel and act as Irishmen! The fact of being placed by God in this land, seemed never to suggest the idea that they were to work for it, or would have to render an account of their stewardship. Men and women are dead and dying around us, whose hearts through life never throbbed at the word "Country." By some strange hallucination they strove by vulgar imitation to transform themselves into English, and then assumed they were identical, though England by many a bitter sarcasm showed how she scorned their pretended claim.'[28]

A poem like 'The Faithless Shepherds' is driven by her anger at the criminal irresponsibility of Irish landlords and she used her poem to warn them of the violent punishment they will inevitably merit. In the words of Karen Tipper, the landlords are depicted in this poem as 'Dead people feeding like noxious, spindly weeds off a dead land':[29]

---

28. Walshe, p. 235.
29. Tipper, p. 204.

> "Os habent, et non loquuntur:
> Oculos habent, et non vident."
> DEAD! – dead! Ye are dead while ye live;
> Ye've a name that ye live – but are dead.
> Neither counsel nor love did ye give,
> And your lips never uttered a word
> While swift ruin downward sped,
> And the plague raged on undisturbed.
> Not a throb of true life in your veins,
> Not a pulse in your passionate heart,
> Not a thought in your dull, cold brains,
> Of how ye should bear your part,
> When summoned the strife to brave,
> For our Country, with Death and the Grave.
> Ye have gold for the follies of fashion,
> And gold for its tinsel glare,
> But none for the wild, sobbing passion
> Wrung from the lips of despair.
> False Shepherds and Guides are ye,
> For the heart in each bosom is cold
> As the ice on a frozen sea;
> And your trappings of velvet and gold
> Lie heavy and close as a pall,
> When the steps of the bearers fall
> On a grave, with measured tread;
> For ye seem to live – but are dead.
> Ye are dead! – ye are dead! stone by stone
> The temple is crumbling down;
> It will fall with a crash of doom,
> For the night deepens dark in its gloom.

Her poems captured much of the public horror at the Famine and her work was greatly admired, but the authorities were unhappy with the general popularity of the *Nation,* particularly the work of a new editor, John Mitchel (1815–1875), whom she disliked and distrusted. Another poem, 'Sign of the Times', written in April 1847, predicts the changes that will happen across Europe and warning the monarchs of Europe that their time is limited:

> On its brow a name is written – France read it once before,
> And like a demon's compact, it was written in her gore–
> A fearful name – thrones trembled as the murmur pass along,
> RETRIBUTION, proud oppressors, for your centuries of wrong.
> From the orient to the ocean, from the palm-tree to the pine,
> From Innisfail, by Tagus, to the lordly Apennine–
> From Indus to the river by which pale Warsaw bleeds,
> Souls are awakening – hands are arming – God is blessing noble deeds.

Jane Wilde's poetry and the vicissitudes of her literary reputation is worth considering with that of other women poets for *The Nation*. For example, Young Irelander 'Eva', Mary Anne Kelly O'Doherty (1830–1910) began contributing to *The Nation* in 1844. 'Eva's' fiancé Kevin O'Doherty was arrested in 1848 and eventually transported and she was vehement in her attack on the government's policy during the Famine. As with Jane Wilde, 'Eva' called for armed rebellion by Irish women and men alike. As Rose Kovak notes, 'In her 1848 address "To the Women of Ireland" published in *The Nation,* Eva O'Doherty insisted upon the propriety of women taking up arms in the cause of Irish independence. 'A coward woman,' she wrote, 'is as base as a coward man. She is bound to act in any situation, just as its circumstances demand. It is not unfeminine to take sword or gun, if sword and gun are required.'[30] As much as Jane Wilde, 'Eva' believed

---

30. Rose Novak, 'Reviving "Eva" of *The Nation?:* Eva O'Doherty's Young Ireland Newspaper Poetry' *Victorian Periodicals Review,* Vol. 45, No. 4 (Winter 2012), pp. 436–465.

in violent action and her poem 'For Ireland All' appeared in *The Nation's* July 1847 issue, seeing Ireland as a mother, gathering her children of all classes and religions to resist the tyranny of the 'English hoof':

> For Ireland all, is the thunder call,
> For Ireland and her salvation:
> Each nerve and thought to her cause be brought,
> In lowly and lofty station.
> Shall the English hoof trample down your roof,
> And tread in your ancient places?[31]

Unlike Jane Wilde, 'Eva' spent much of her time in Galway during this time of Famine and was thus able to observe the suffering of the country people, and wrote to protest government distribution of inadequate and ill-prepared food and she published a satirical poem, 'Down Britannia,' a mocking version of 'Rule Britannia' in June 1884. Later, 'Eva' was to move to Australia in 1860 to marry her fiancé and she continued to publish poems on exile and on loss. Eventually, she published her Young Ireland poems in 1877, with some revisions. Later, during the era of the Celtic revival, the Dublin publisher M.H. Gill published a new volume of her *Nation* poems, with many of her more militant poems left out. 'Eva's' stature as a writer waned in her lifetime and seemed to have depended on the context of the revolutionary years of 1848 and the rebellion. In contrast, Jane Wilde continued to strengthen her public profile with her translations, her folklore collecting and her essays. Novak suggests that 'In O'Doherty's case, the neutralisation of her radicalism in the 1909 edition of her poems resulted in a sentimentalised representation of her former role as a militant Irish nationalist and effaced an important moment in the history of the Irish press.'[32] Novak goes to note that 'Wilde's

---

31. Ibid., p. 443.
32. Novak, p. 457.

writing differs from O'Doherty's in several ways. Unlike that of O'Doherty, Wilde's work was shaped by her admiration of German romantic nationalism and her attraction to Thomas Carlyle's neo-feudalism. Wilde's work thus demonstrates her advocacy of violent revolutionary nationalism, but it also reveals an apprehension regarding popular revolution and democracy, whereas O'Doherty's Young Ireland poetry reveals a strong republican voice that elicits sympathy for agrarian insurgency and popular mobilisation.'[33] This comparison with 'Eva' of *The Nation* is a useful one. It is clear that the radicalism of *The Nation* period did not endure for the other women writers. For Jane Wilde, her facility to adapt and diversify ensure the longevity of the literary reputation with her lifetime and the survival of a very limited range of her work after her death.

When Jane Wilde came to publish her collected poems in 1864, *Poems by Speranza* with a Dublin publisher, James Duffy, as 'Speranza (Lady Wilde),' she dedicated the collection to her two sons with the words, "I made them indeed speak plain the word COUNTRY,/ I taught them, no doubt, that a country's a thing men should die for.' (As it turned out, neither son showed much interest in Irish nationalism in their subsequent careers, never mind dying for it.) This same collection was reissued in a second edition in 1870 with a Glasgow publisher Cameron and Ferguson and a new dedication, *To Ireland, My Country /Wounded at the Heart.*' In both editions, Jane Wilde choses to open with her poems from her time writing for *The Nation,* with 'The Brothers' and 'The Famine Year' and she chose other key writings on the Famine, like 'A Lament for the Potato' AD 1739.'[34] It is not a translation as Jane Wilde had little direct knowledge of Irish but she had access to dictionaries and indeed scholars of the Irish

---

33. Ibid., note 17, p. 459.
34. Translation from the Irish preserved in a manuscript in the hand of John O'Daly (a nineteenth-century scholar). I wish to thank Eleanor Fitzsimons for this information.

language and this is her version:

> There is woe, there is clamour, in our desolated land,
> And wailing lamentation from a Famine-stricken band;
> And weeping are the multitudes in sorrow and despair,
> For the green fields of Munster lying desolate and bare.
> Woe for Lorc's ancient kingdom, sunk in slavery and grief;
> Plundered, ruined, are our gentry, our people, and their Chief;
> For the harvest lieth scattered, more worth to us than gold,
> All the kindly food that nourished both the young and the old.
> Well I mind me of the cosherings, where princes might dine,
> And we drank until nightfall the best seven sorts of wine;
> Yet was ever the Potato our old, familiar dish,
> And the best of all sauces with the beeves and the fish.
> But the harp now is silent, no one careth for the sound;
> No flowers, no sweet honey, and no beauty can be found;
> Not a bird its music thrilling through the leaves of the wood,
> Nought but weeping and hands wringing in despair for our food.

In the second edition, she adds in later poems, like her memorial poems for William Carleton and for Daniel O'Connell and 'Have We Done Well for Ireland', a poem written after the end of the 1848, questioning if real peace had been achieved and what lay lurking in the future:

> 'But now, ye say, the Land hath rest –
> Aye, with the death weights on her eyes;
> And fettered arms across her breast,
> And mail'd hands stifling down her cries.
> So rests a corpse within the grave
> O'er which the charnel grasses wave.

Oh, better far some kindly word
To stay the vengeance-lifted sword,
Or Love, with queenly, outstretched hand,
To soothe thee – fated Ireland!'

Jane Wilde wrote widely on Spanish literature and so she went to a defining moment in Spanish history for her poem, 'The Fall of the Tyrants,' a dramatic rendering of the capture of Granada by the Catholic Spanish monarchs Isabella and Ferdinand, in 1492. This was when the last bastion of Moorish rule was taken and the Alhambra fell into Christian hand, ending centuries of Arab rule in Spain and particularly in Andalusia:

Ho! Spaniards! rise for Liberty—your country on ye calls,
To fight to-day, in proud array, before Granáda's walls;
A proud array is here to-day, full fifty thousand strong,
Of Fantassins and Cavaliers Gonzalo leads along.

From Leon to Granáda—from Corunna to Севílle,
Gather, Spaniards, gather, by the banks of the Xenil!
Eight hundred years of blood and tears beneath a foreign sway
Eight hundred years of blood and tears must be avenged to-day.
And, mountaineers, have ye no tears to be avenged to-day
Asturians, and Gallicians, and wild dwellers by Vizcày?
Ye, the unconquered remnant of the brave old Celtic race
For ne'er could Roman, Goth, or Moor, your nationhood efface.
Now, now, oh, shame and misery! a stranger rules your lands!
A stranger's spoil is your native soil—a stranger's voice commands;
Ye, princes once and chieftains, ere the false foe crossed the flood,

Now, drawers of their water and base hewers of their wood!
And, Andalusian Brothers, of the old Vandalic race,
Will ye alone 'midst Spaniards, be proud of your disgrace?
They flatter, fawn, but hate you, these proud foes to whom you've sold
Your Liberty for mocking smiles—your country for their gold.

They own your stately palaces, they desecrate your shrines,
They trample on your vineyards, yet ye stoop to drink their wines;
Ye wear their silk, their gold, their gems, and to their feasts ye run;
Now shame for ye, my brothers, is it thus that Freedom's won?

No coward fears—eight hundred years ye've lived as slaves, not men;
But swords makes bright each chartered right—ye'll have your own again.
Brave hearts and leal of proud Castile—Revenge, on Mauritania!
Rend earth and sky with your gathering cry: Charge! Cierra España!

In this poem she takes the view that the fall of the Moorish kingdom of Granada was a victory for the Celtic races: 'Ye, the unconquered remnant of the brave old Celtic race/For ne'er could Roman, Goth, or Moor, your nationhood effaces.' Most of Spain had been conquered and subdued by the Moors, except for Galicia, a region seen as purely Celtic. Thus, in this poem, she sees the final conquest of Granada as a parallel victory for a Christian, Celtic people over an oppressive foreign invading force, vanquished after centuries of occupation. This was not always the way in which her Spanish counterparts viewed the fall of Granada, indeed many poets and writers in Andalusia lamented the loss of the Moorish civilisation and the imposition of Catholicism. Jane Wilde always interprets European historical parallels from the prism of Irish suffering under the yoke of British rule.

The Trial of *The Nation*

All this explosive poetry finally provoked a reaction from the British authorities when Charles Gavan Duffy were arrested on 15th July 1848. He continued to write from prison and to correspond with Jane Wilde. When the police arrested Duffy, they raided the office of *The Nation,* smashed up the type and removed all seditious materials. However, Duffy's cousin Margaret Callan (1817–1883) took over the running of the journal while Habeas Corpus was suspended throughout Ireland and martial law introduced. In these dangerous times, Jane Wilde herself became editor of *The Nation* in July 1848, and Duffy asked her to write an editorial. On July 22, 1848, she published 'The Challenge to Ireland' in which she put the question 'And are there no men in your Fatherland /to confront the tyrant's stormy glare.'

This editorial was Jane Wilde's most sustained call to arms and the text that would provoke the court case where she became the centre of public scrutiny. She faced down such scrutiny with aplomb and a real sense of dramatic composure. As we can see below, her impassioned call for armed rebellion has a vitality and a rhetorical power that alarmed the British authorities and still has a thrilling energy.

> Oh! for a hundred thousand muskets glittering brightly in the light of heaven, and the monumental barricades stretching across each of our noble streets, made desolate by England – circling around that doomed Castle [Dublin Castle, seat of British administration in Ireland], made

infamous by England, where the foreign tyrant has held his council of treason and iniquity against our people and our country for seven hundred years. Courage rises with danger and heroism with resource. Does not our breath come freer, each heartbeat quicker in these rare and grand moments of human life when all doubt and wavering and weakness are cast to the winds and the soul rises majestic over each petty obstacle, each low, petty consideration and fling off the fetters of prejudice, bigotry and egotism bounds forward into the higher diviner life of heroism and patriotism, defiant as a conqueror, devoted as a martyr, omnipotent as a deity. We appeal to the whole Irish Nation – is there any man amongst us who wishes to take one further step on the base path of sufferance and slavery? Is there one man who thinks that Ireland has not been sufficiently insulted, that Ireland has not been sufficiently degraded in her honour and her rights to justify now in fiercely turning upon her oppressor? No! A man so infamous cannot tread the earth; or, if he does, the voice of the coward is stifled in clear, wild, ringing shout that leaps from hill to hill, that echoes from sea to sea, that peals from the lips of an uprising nation, we must be free.[35]

The powerful language, the call for rebellion, the insistence of a common ground for all classes and religions in Ireland places her work firmly within the tradition of Irish republican speech making. This essay, like many of the graveside orations or the courtroom speeches, locates a moment in the discourse of Irish republican resistance, where sacrifice and necessary violence are given a divine or God-given aspect. This is the transformative moment, rebellion becoming sanctified by the nobility of death. In this, Jane Wilde is aligning herself with the traditions of Irish republicanism and setting a tone for many of the poets and the writers of the later

---

35. *The Nation*, July 1848. See Walshe, *Selected Writings of Speranza and William Wilde*, p. 53.

Celtic Revival and for the leaders of the 1916 Easter Rising. She was also fulfilling her perceived role as educator/poet, undoing the neglect of British rule in relation to public knowledge and understanding with her creative powers:

> In the name then of your trampled, insulted, degraded country; in the name of all heroic virtues, of all that man's life illustrious or death divine, in the name of your starved, your exiled, your dead; by your martyrs in prison cells and felon chains; in the name of God and man; by the listening earth and the watching heaven, I call on you to make this aspiration of your souls a *deed*. Even as you read these weak words of a heart that not yet palpitates with an enthusiasm as heroic as your own and your breast heaves as your eyes grow dim with tears, as the memory of Ireland's wrongs rushed upon your soul – even now lift your right hand to swear – swear by your undying soul, by your hopes of immortality, never to lay down your arms, never to cease hostilities, till you regenerate and save this fallen land.
>
> [...] One bold, one decisive move. One instant to take breath, and then a rising; a rush, a charge from north, south, east, and west upon the English garrison, and the land is ours. Do your eyes flash, do your hearts throb at the prospect of having a country? For you have had no country. You have never felt the pride, the dignity, the majesty of independence. You could never lift your head to heaven and glory in the name of Irishman, for all Europe read the brand of slave upon your brow.[36]

This call to arms created a sensation. Karen Tipper has identified the force of these words in invoking a rhetorical lineage for the Young Irelanders in these terms: 'In "Jacta Alea Est," besides

---

36. Ibid., pp. 54–55.

justifying the insurrection, Jane Wilde reinforces the principles taught over the years in *The Nation*. She calls on the descendants of heroes, martyrs and sufferers to cast aside all doubts and let their intellects triumph over their own sins of selfishness, bigotry and distrust which create triumph over tyranny and oppression.'[37]

Her words seemed to have immediate results for a country on the verge of rebellion. At the end of July, an uprising took place in south Tipperary, where some of the more militant of the Young Irelanders came into armed conflict with the Royal Irish Constabulary, resulting in hostage-taking at the farm of a local woman, a widow called Mc Cormack. The rebellion soon petered out and the farcical nature of this one moment of armed conflict was known derisively as the Battle of Widow McCormack's Cabbage Patch. Leaders like Thomas Francis Meagher and others were arrested in August 1848 and put on trial. All of them were convicted of high treason and sentenced to death but eventually they were deported, as the British government were unwilling to create new political martyrs by executing them. Meagher was transported to Tasmania in 1849 but soon escaped to America where he fought in the American Civil War, and was later appointed Governor of Montana.

The next trial of significance came in February 1849, when Charles Gavan Duffy was brought before the courts for publishing that seditious call to arms and held responsible for the offending article. Jane Wilde wanted to take responsibility for her editorial and even went to see the Solicitor General in his office to confess her authorship, but the trial went ahead without her being arrested. Her authorship of the editorial was an open secret but, as *The Freeman's Journal* stated, that there was 'No way of proving the authorship remained but by producing the lady herself upon the table – a course Mr Duffy peremptorily refused to take.'[38] She was reported to have stood up in the body of the court during

---
37. Tipper, p. 219.
38. O'Sullivan, p. 54.

the trail and declared loudly, 'I am the culprit, if culprit there be.'[39] However, it was said that the judge refused to listen to her and thus *The Nation* trial fell apart and the charges against Duffy dropped. In a letter to her Scottish friend John Hilson, Jane Wilde wrote that 'I think this piece of Heroism will make a good scene when I write my Life.'[40] Her legend as Speranza was taking shape.

Retrospectively, Speranza's moment in the courtroom would come to be viewed as part of a nineteenth-century sequence of Irish nationalist moments of resistance against British imperial justice, from Robert Emmet to Thomas Francis Meagher and onwards to Pearse in the early twentieth century. Seamus Heaney saw Jane Wilde as an Irish patriot standing up to the iniquities of British justice with style, as he outlines in his 1995 essay 'Speranza in Reading Gaol'.[41] In his dedication speech in Westminster Abbey on 14 February 1995, Heaney takes up this theme again, seeing the Wilde family as immersed in this tradition of republican resistance writing:

> The cry of hurt is every bit as audible in the *Ballad of Reading Gaol* as it is in the song of St James's Infirmary although the provenance of Wilde's chain-gang poem is Irish rather than American and looks back to all the convict ballads, gaol journals and political poetry of Irish nationalist literature in the nineteenth-century – a literature in which Wilde's mother famously contributed under the pseudonym of Speranza.[42]

The failure of the rebellion and the sense that the moment for

---

39. Melville, p 39.
40. Letter to John Hilson, April 1849, University of Reading Special Collections, MS 559.
41. Seamus Heaney, 'Speranza in Reading Gaol' in *The Redress of Poetry* (London: Faber and Faber, 1995), p. 95.
42. Seamus Heaney, 'Oscar Wilde dedication: Westminster Abbey, 14 February 1995', in *Wilde the Irishman*, ed. Jerusha McCormack (New Haven, CT: Yale University Press, 1998), pp. 174–75.

freedom and change had passed meant that Jane Wilde felt somewhat disillusioned. After this close brush with British justice, she continued writing of her anger against British rule in Ireland, even when she became an established and respected figure within Irish literary circles and, paradoxically, still very much welcome in the official circles of the British Administration. Later she wrote to John Hilson, with some glee, that 'I went to the last drawing room at the castle and Lord Aberdeen smiled very archly as he bent to kiss my cheek, which is the ceremony of presentation. I smiled too and thought of "Jacta Alea Est".'[43]

This idea of being both part of the establishment, a welcome figure in Dublin Castle and a writer of revolutionary prose was part of the enjoyment for her. As Emer O'Sullivan has written 'She stepped into the limelight and became a public figure. She was established as a paradox: a Protestant nationalist, a bourgeois rebel. A revolutionary who was excessively an ease in the bosom of the Establishment.'[44] Paradox was something that Jane Wilde thrived on and she enjoyed inhabiting ambivalent spaces in her writing and in her public and private life.

Daniel O'Connell

In his later years, O'Connell fell out of favour with younger revolutionaries and was judged as a failure, compromising his earlier promise. As Karen Tipper writes, 'During the years in which she wrote for *The Nation,* Jane Wilde too viewed O'Connell unfavourably, contrasting his character and performance with the pure devotion and noble deeds of earlier heroes and of her own colleagues who risked failure rather than compromise their values. Later she was to become more circumspect and more conservative in her views.'[45] The moment of O'Connell's death in 1847 was one

---

43. Melville, p. 40.
44. O'Sullivan, p. 56.
45. Tipper, p. 118.

of great emotion for Ireland, as the Great Famine of 1845–8 had been a source of heartbreak and sorrow for the dying O'Connell and his death a sad one. O'Connell left Ireland in January 1847 and set out on pilgrimage to Rome. However, he never made it to Rome and instead died on the way, in Genoa in May 1847. Jane Wilde's dedicatory poem 'O'Connell' was published in *The Nation* at a time when O'Connell's body, minus his heart, which was sent to Rome for burial, was returned for burial in Glasnevin Cemetery in Dublin, beneath a Round Tower.

> Crowned with a liberated people's love,
> Crowned by the Nations with eternal fame,
> His great heart burning still with patriot-fire,
> Tho' Death's pale shadow rested on his brow,
> Forth went the mighty Chief from his loved Land,
> 'Mid the hushed reverence paid to dying Kings,
> On his last pilgrimage, yearning to find rest
> For the o'erwearied hero-heart and brain,
> After great trials pass'd and triumphs won,
> Within the Temple-City of the World.
> But, faint with combats of a glorious life,
> Tho' Freedom's hymns still murmured on his lips,
> And his dim eyes still tracked the western Sun
> Would rise in Ireland, but no more for him,
> Seeking the gates of God's great Church on earth,
> He found the gates of Heaven, and entered in
> There Angels met him with the conqueror's Palm,
> And passing from the portal to the Throne,
> Circled with golden glitter of their wings,
> God crowned him Victor for his work well done!

Her poem is unusual in that she, unlike many of her contemporaries, recognised the compromises forced on him his later political career and was sympathetic to the limitations and the disappointments of his final years. She saw his passing as a real moment of loss and sorrow for Ireland and recognised the ways in which he had been disappointed and wounded by the trauma of the Famine.

Her full-length essay on O'Connell was later published in her collection, *Men, Women and Books,* full of admiration for his democratic impulses, his horror of armed rebellion and mob violence. 'He knew that Irish independence could never be achieved by epileptic fits of mad ferocity.'[46] Jane Wilde makes the shrewd point that he held sway by the fact that the Irish are, as she puts it, 'genuine hero-worshippers' and that 'it was through their affections, far more than their interests, that O'Connell attained such imperial sway.'[47] To some extent, Jane Wilde is condescending in her description of the Catholic working class as 'unfitted for the heroic virtues which a republic demands,'[48] yet it could be argued that she was simply stating an unpalatable truth that British rule has sapped civic responsibility and spirit from the Irish populace. She concludes by seeing 'the glory that rests on the brow of him who fought and suffered to elevate a degraded and despairing people will never be effaced, for the light is consecrated to immortality on the page of history and in the heat of an emancipated nation.'[49] Her assessment of O'Connell stands out with her fairmindedness and sense of fair play and this despite her own impulses towards armed revolution and the urgent call for Irish rebels to take to action.

Years later, Jane Wilde was to publish an essay on that period of her life called 'Irish Leaders and Martyrs' in which she celebrated her part in this exciting generation of activists. What she most admired was

---

46. Jane Wilde, *Men, Women and Books,* p. 196.
47. Ibid., p.185.
48. Ibid., p. 195.
49. Ibid., p. 197.

> The fervent nationality evoked by Moore's music and song at the opening of the century and formulated afterwards into an immense political force by O'Connell, rose to a fever of enthusiasm in 1848, when a madness of lyrical passion seemed to sweep over the heart of the nation, and "Young Ireland" sprang to manhood, splendid in force and intellect, earnest in aim, and stainless in life and act.[50]

For a woman who was keenly aware of the subordinate roles forced on politically active women like herself, she still was very much part of a male generation. Yet she never comments directly on this, enumerating instead a list of male activists: 'Amongst the new band of workers were powerful organisers like Gavan Duffy; chivalrous leaders like Smith O'Brien, orators like Dillon and Meagher; and fervent apostles of freedom like John Mitchel, one of the boldest, bravest, and most noble-hearted of patriots. But the man, above all, whose words were a tocsin of Revolution, was the poet, orator and leader, Thomas Davis.'[51] Her belief in the poetic achievements of her generation was explicitly linked to their national identity, a belief that saw Celticism as an all-embracing and unifying identity for the diverse classes and sectarian identities in Ireland. 'For Celtic favour always finds its fullest expression in oratory and song.'[52] This was to influence her later sense that the Celtic imagination could provide an inclusive aesthetic for Irish cultural nationalists. Her sense of pride in her part in this vital and exciting generations of poets and orators remained with her for the rest of her life and she remembered the men of her generation with reverence and affection. However, this essay ends on a melancholic note, with her conclusion that all these men died unhappy or unfulfilled men, and that her generation was a doomed one because of the tyranny of British rule:

---

50. Walshe, *Selected Writings of Speranza and William Wilde*, p. 241.
51. Ibid., p. 248.
52. Walshe, *Selected Writings of Speranza and William Wilde*, p. 247.

> Yet, the fate of many of those who made '48 a splendid moment in Irish history, was dark and tragic, and the flame lit up by patriot-passion died out in martyrdom.... A natural result when there is no kinship or sympathy between the rulers and the ruled, no pride of race, no heroic memories, no traditions of suffering common to both, yet the word country should be for ever sacred, and lie at the base of all individual action and effort; for love of country is the divine force that can alone war against the degrading tendencies of mere material gain; and no mental or moral elevation can be attained by a people who do not, above all, and before all, things, uphold and reverence the hold rights of their Motherland.[53]

After all this excitement, she continued to publish, with her poems starting to appear from 1849 in the *Dublin University Magazine*. This important literary and political magazine had been founded in Dublin, 1833 and was to continue until 1882 and she published there as Speranza during the 1840s and then as Lady Wilde up to her departure to London. Originally founded as a journal noted for political commentary, it was a prestigious and worthwhile platform for her writings. In addition, *The Nation* relaunched in September 1849.

Sidonia The Sorceress (1849)

Her first full-length book was a translation of the fictionalised version of the life of Sidonia von Borcke, by the Pomeranian priest and author J. W Meinhold, published in German in 1847. Jane Wilde published her anonymous two-volume version in 1849, keeping her name from the title page. The original novel was inspired by the real-life Sidonia von Borcke, a Pomeranian noblewoman and landowner a sub prioress at a Lutheran abbey

---
53. Ibid., pp. 246–8.

who was burned in 1620 as a witch in Stettin for her supposed crimes of murder and sexual contact with the devil. Her translation is pacey and lively, a full account of the ways in which the evil Sidonia seduces and murders to her heart's content, dancing on graves, torturing geese and eventually to die suitably punished.

Michael Cronin comments that she 'maintains the energy, vigour and gorgeousness of the original in her translation as can be seen above. Unlike her poetry translation for *The Nation*, she leaves aside the rhetorical and the flaccid for more direct forms of expression which make Sidonia an unforgettable character in English. Elgee [Jane Wilde] avoids a ponderousness in form that was often the fate that befell German translation in English in the nineteenth century. She does not bowdlerise an account that would be considered sensational reading matter for a mid-nineteenth-century public in the English-speaking world.'[54]

It was a dramatic story and as can be seen from this extract, she rendered it with wit and vigour:

> After that, he fell into disrepute with the old nobility, for which he cared little, seeing that his riches and magnificence always secured him companions enough, who were willing to listen to his wisdom, and were consoled by his wine. As to Otto, no one observed any sign of repentance in him. On the contrary, he seemed to glory in his crime, and the neighbouring nobles related that he frequently brought his little daughter Sidonia, whom he adored for her beauty, to the assembled guests, magnificently attired; and when she was bowing to the company, he would say, "Who art thou, my little daughter?" then she would cease the salutations which she had learned from her mother, and drawing herself up, proudly exclaim, "I am a noble maiden, dowered with towns and castles!" Then he would ask, if the conversation

---

54. Cronin, p. 18.

turned upon his enemies – and half the nobles were so – "Sidonia, how does thy father treat his enemies?" Upon which the child would straighten her finger, and running at her father, strike it into his heart, saying, "*Thus* he treats them." At which Otto would laugh loudly and tell her to show him how the knave looked when he was dying. Then Sidonia would fall, twist her face, and writhe her little hands and feet in horrible contortions. Upon which Otto would lift her up and kiss her upon the mouth. But it will be seen how the just God punished him for all this, and how the words of the Scriptures were fulfilled: "Err not, God is not mocked; for what a man soweth, that shall he also reap."[55]

Karen Tipper writes that 'Jane Wilde herself considered the work simply an exercise, the first serious challenge to her translating ability and certainly not a novel for which she felt any affinity.'[56] This is to underestimate the importance of her first book. The story of Sidonia was an influence on Dante Gabriel Rossetti, who read Jane Wilde's translation in 1851 and pronounced it a masterpiece. The cultural influence of her translation continued, as Edward Burne-Jones painted on the theme, Charlotte Brontë read it, and references it in her novel *Villette* and also Walter Pater writes of it, as did Swinburne. Tipper quotes from Edmund Gosse who wrote, 'How the attention of Speranza was directed to it, I am quite unable to report, but it is hardly a paradox to say that this German romance did not begin to exist until an Irishwoman revealed it to a select English circle.'[57] Her son Oscar said it was his favourite book as a child!

She continued her interest in French literature with the Lamartine translations she produced in 1850 and 1851, the first work entitled in English, *Pictures of the First French Revolution* (Lamartine 1850).

---

55. Walshe, *Selected Writings of Speranza and William Wilde*, p. 63.
56. Tipper, pp. 361–2.
57. Ibid., p. 363.

This was her translation of Lamartine's *L'Histoire des Girondins* (1847), written as revolutionary opposition to the regime of Louis-Philippe. Alphonse de Lamartine was a revolutionary, later becoming Minister for Foreign Affairs in February 1848 but his political fortunes sank with the establishment of the Second Empire under Napoleon III. From 1851 onwards, he no longer played an active role in political life and there seems to have been some correspondence between Jane Wilde and Lamartine.[58] As in the case of the Meinhold translation, her name did not appear on the title page of *Pictures*.

---

58. I am grateful to Merlin Holland for this information on Lamartine.

CHAPTER THREE

Merrion Square (1851–1879)

Number One, Merrion Square was Jane Wilde's home from 1853 until her move to London in May 1879. The physical location of this impressive Georgian house, one of the finest in Dublin, was indicative of her place within Irish cultural and political life. Merrion Square was where many of Ireland's leading figures lived, including the novelist Sheridan LeFanu, and indeed Daniel O'Connell had spent time there. Merrion Square also later became the home of W.B. Yeats. (Presently, Merrion Square is the site of a celebrated statue of her son Oscar, but it took well over a century after her death for Jane Wilde's connection with Merrion Square to be officially acknowledged by a plaque on the house.) Here, Jane Wilde could connect with the leading intellectuals of the time. Her regular Saturday afternoon salon allowed her to continue her public role as poet and to encourage younger writers throughout her time in this house, one of the finest in Dublin. This was the longest time she spent at one address and so in this section, the focus is on her literary and social life in Merrion Square and on the intellectual and creative partnership with her husband, William Wilde.

At this period, salons were of course important places for the maintenance of an enduring professional life for the writer, providing, as Caoilfhionn Ní Bheacháin and Angus Mitchel note in their study of London salon culture, 'fertile ground for intellectual exchange, and for cultural and political ferment [...] and an important conduit for ideas, sentiments and dispositions.'[1] Her life, and the network of relationships Jane Wilde maintained through her gatherings in Merrion Square, were very closely linked with her husband William Wilde and, by the time they married, both were already noted scholars and writers. It is not clear exactly how they met, but they had been part of the same literary and intellectual circles in Dublin, as indicated by Jane's admiring review of his work, and William quotes one of her verses in his 1849 book, *Boyne and Blackwater*. Jane Wilde's mother had recently died and so, when they were married on 12th November 1851, it was a low-key affair and she temporarily shed her mourning clothes for the ceremony. After a wedding trip to England, they both went to live in William's house at nearby 21, Westland Row, moving to Merrion Square in 1853 after the birth of their sons Willie and Oscar. The intellectual relationship between Jane and William Wilde was important to her writing and her publications.

An antiquarian and oculist, William Wilde was already a renowned medical scientist and travel writer. He was born in Castlerea, County Roscommon, in 1815, and began his medical training in Dublin at an early age specialising as an aurist and oculist. Then, in 1837, he toured the Levant in charge of an invalid patient, Robert Meikle, a member of the Royal Yacht Squadron. The resulting account of the trip, his first travel book, was an immediate success and established his reputation as a writer. In 1844, he founded the St. Mark's Ophthalmic Hospital in Dublin, spending over one thousand pounds of his own money, while working at a lucrative and demanding private medical practice. This medical practice was to fund the couple's lifestyle in Merrion Square and allow them both to become generous and popular hosts to the writers and scientists of their day. At the same time, William

---

1. C. Ní Bheacháin and A. Mitchel. 'Alice Stopford Green and Vernon Lee: Salon Culture and Intellectual Exchange', *Journal of Victorian Culture*, 25:1 (2020), pp. 77–94.

Wilde published on medicine, Irish antiquities, and general literature. His energy and drive meant that, by the age of thirty, he was a member of the Imperial Society of Physicians in Vienna and by 1853 had published another successful travel book, this time on Austria. His *Boyne and Blackwater* was published in 1850, also to great acclaim. He had also become one of the most active members of the Royal Irish Academy, creating the first catalogues of their collections and crucially involved in the activities of their work in archaeology. William was passionate about his learning and his scholarship and was capable of argument and of debate. At one point, he resigned from the Royal Irish Academy, angry at the paucity of their grant to help him catalogue their collections, but they were soon reconciled and he resumed his work.

Another unconventional aspect to his life was the fact that William Wilde had a son and two daughters born before his marriage. His son, who went by the name of Henry Wilson, was 13 years old when his father married, and was trained by him to become an ophthalmologist. He later became his father's partner in his medical practice and lived nearby on Merrion Square. Recent research surmises that the mother of Henry Wilson was a cousin of William Wilde, Emily Finn (1804–1884). Emily Finn may have been a relation of William Wilde's mother, who was also a Finn. Emily was born in Mayo, where she married a man called Charles Cromie, had a daughter with him and later separated from him, moving to Dublin. Emily Cromie was thirty-four when Henry Wilson was born in 1838, at a time when William Wilde was on his Levantine tour and would outlive both Henry Wilson and William Wilde, dying in 1884. As recounted later in this chapter, Oscar Wilde tells of a woman in a dark veil who came and visited his father on his deathbed, brought into his bedroom by Jane Wilde herself; this woman may have been Emily Cromie, William's cousin and possibly the mother of his son.[2] His

---

2. Fergus O'Connor, 'Henry Wilson, Half-Brother of Oscar Wilde.' *The Wildean* 52 (2022), pp. 24–37. I am grateful to Eleanor Fitzsimons for this information.

daughters Mary and Emily were born two and four years before Jane and William married and they lived in Monaghan with his brother Ralph, a clergyman, who acted as their guardian. Nothing is known of their mother. Henry Wilson was very much part of the Wilde family and when he died, he left some money to Willie and Oscar and to Emily Cromie and her daughter. Jane Wilde clearly knew and accepted William's children.

This unconventionality was widely known in Dublin and meant that, as public figures, neither of them was afraid of debate and of taking apparently contradictory positions. What is clear is that their intellectual interests had already run parallel before they had met. During their marriage, his experience as an archaeologist and folklore collector complimented her interest in Irish cultural nationalism. They both felt the urgency to preserve an endangered Irish folk imagination and their imaginative use of their research into folklore was to be transformative for the literature of Irish cultural nationalism later in the nineteenth century. They both drew from the same body of learning on early Irish cultures and legends and deployed this learning as a resistance to the British Empire.

William had first-hand experience of the Irish Famine of the mid-1840s in his role as a doctor. As we saw, in her poems, Jane Wilde wrote of the dire consequences of this Famine with immediacy and terror, urging resistance, rebellion, outright revolution. At the same time, often using his own money, William worked hard to catalogue vanishing Irish historical artefacts and to preserve vital archaeological and folkloric traditions on the verge of extinction. It was clearly a partnership based on respect for each other's stature and learning, as well as affection and loyalty. William Wilde's areas of research were also to connect with Jane's interests in Irish cultural nationalism and his folklore collecting, published in 1852 as *Irish Popular Superstitions,* would influence her later publications on Irish folktales and superstitions. Her dedication to her writing was paralleled by his passion for science. In a letter to her friend

MERRION SQUARE (1851–1879)

John Hilson in Scotland, in 1852, the year after she married, she describes William as 'a celebrity – a man eminent in his profession, of acute intellect and much learning, the best conversationalist in our metropolis, in short he is a man to be proud of as far as intellect goes.' She goes on, with characteristic honesty, to allude to his

> strange, hypochondriacal home nature which the world never sees [...] when I ask him what could make him happy, he answers death and yet the next hour if any excitement arouses him he will throw himself into the rush of life, as if life were eternal here. His whole existence is one of unceasing mental activity.[3]

This vivid account of William Wilde's singular personality, his moments of despair, depression and energy, provide an invaluable insight to their lives together and the ways in which they inspired each other in their writings.

Their marriage was, overall, a successful one, based on mutual respect and weathering the loss of their beloved daughter, the existence of William's natural-born children before he married and the scandal of a court case for libel. Their children, Willie, Oscar, and Isola were born over the next years. She wrote to John Hilson:

> Joan of Arc was never meant for marriage, and so here I am, bound heart and soul to the home hearth by the tiny hands of my little Willie and as if these sweet hands were not enough, behold me – me, Speranza – also rocking a cradle at this present writing in which lies my second son – a babe of one month old the 16th of this month and as large and fine and handsome and healthy as if he were three months. He is to be called Oscar Fingal Wilde. Is not that grand, misty and Ossianic?

---

3. Karen Tipper, *Lady Jane Wilde's Letters to Mr. John Higson, 1847–1876* (New York: Edwin Mellen, 2010), p. 56.

She mentions her children frequently in her correspondence and, although she wrote, with a kind of mock lament 'Alas the fates are cruel, Behold Speranza making gruel',[4] she loved her children dearly and made sure they shared to the full the very lively atmosphere in Merrion Square and at their home in the West of Ireland. With the money he made, in 1853 William bought a fishing lodge in Connemara on the shores of Lough Fee to pursue his interest in folklore and archaeology and for the family to enjoy their summers.

Jane Wilde continued to write and to translate with unabated skill and energy in her married life, with translations of *Pictures of the French Revolution* published in 1850, *The Wanderer* in 1851 and *The Glacier Land* by Alexandre Dumas Père in 1852, a translation of his lively and idiosyncratic account of Switzerland in 1832. *The First Temptation* by 1863 was a three-volume philosophical romance by the German novelist, Wilhelmine Canz (1815–1901) published in London in 1863. In the novel, the central character, Robert attempts to undermine his wife Elizabeth's faith in God, but all of his efforts are in vain and eventually she is saved and vindicated while he is lost and damned. A review of her translation in *The Athenaeum* was blunt as to the merits of the novel: 'This work is extremely well translated but few readers will have the patience to wade through three thick volumes of German philosophy.'[5] She didn't make a great deal of money from her translations but this was her main literary work during this time. She wrote for the *Dublin Magazine* on Calderón, praising his bloodthirsty lyrical dramas, and an essay on her Elgee cousin, Robert McClure, (1807–1873) in the *Dublin University Magazine*. This cousin, who was born in their grandfather Archdeacon Elgee's house in Wexford, had become a Vice-Admiral in the Royal Navy and was the first to navigate the Northwest Passage while he commanded HMS *Investigator* in 1850, also circumnavigating

---

4. Melville, p. 57.
5. Melville, p. 57.

the Americas during a three-year voyage. (There is no evidence of any direct contact between Jane Wilde and Robert McClure but, by coincidence, they both ended up buried in Kensal Green Cemetery in London.) Her productivity was also evident with two new poems published in *Duffy's Magazine* in 1864, 'Work While It is Called Today' and' Who Will Shew Us Any Good?'

Family life continued to prosper when, in 1862, the Wildes built four houses in Bray, leasing three of them for one hundred and twenty pounds a year and keeping the other one furnished for themselves, as a summer retreat for their young children. In the same year, a much bigger project came to fruition when they built a large country house called Moytura on land bought from William's grandfather's estate on Lough Corrib in County Mayo. William designed the house and called it after the ancient mythical battle of Moytura, involving the Tuatha Dé Danann, which was said to have taken place there, retaining the historical tower standing close by.

Jane's stature as a leading poet was reinforced when she published a collection called *Poems by Speranza* in 1864 and dedicated to her two sons. It was reviewed in *The Freeman's Journal* on 8th December 1864 where the poems lauded for 'the beauty of their imagery, their truthfulness to nature and the purity and simplicity of the phraseology in which our gifted countrywoman conveys her musings.'[6] The editor of *the Irish People*, the novelist Charles Kickham (1828–1882), was himself a devotee of *The Nation* and a member of the Irish Republican Brotherhood, but he gave her collected poems a surprisingly negative review. *The Irish People* had already published a damning review of her poem, 'Who Will Shew Us Any Good' saying 'We scarcely know whether we rightly understand its meaning.'[7] In the May edition in 1864, Charles Kickham, in a nasty move, decided to rewrite some of her poems as prose, to highlight what he saw as the faults of her work. Readers rallied around Jane Wilde to defend her from this

---

6. O'Sullivan, p. 114.
7. Melville, p. 86.

high-handed treatment and one man wrote to say that 'Instead of carping at her productions, we should build her a statue.'[8] This collection was to be re-issued in 1870 and attests to the continued support and enthusiasm for her poems in her lifetime from many, if not all, readers.

Fröken Lotten von Kræmer

Jane Wilde made one of her most important friendships when, in July 1857, Baron Robert von Kræmer, the governor of Uppsala in Sweden, came to Dublin with his daughter Lotten to consult with William about a recurring discomfort in her ears and chronic pain. (She was eventually to lose her hearing.) Lotten von Kræmer (1828–1912) was a poet, essayist, and the editor of a Swedish journal of modern literature and culture called *Our Time*. The daughter and father were invited to dine in Merrion Square, where they were entertained with a concert of Thomas Moore's songs. A firm and long-lasting friendship was the result of this first encounter. Lotten herself wrote an account of the visit in an article entitled 'Oscar Wilde's family home in Ireland's capital.'[9] Jane Wilde proved to be an attentive and scrupulous host for her new Swedish friends: 'We now embarked, in the pleasurable company of Mrs. Wilde, on the outing which her husband had so animatedly prepared for us. And it was clear that we found her to be well-versed in the sights of Dublin, whether it was museums, libraries or churches or those elegant shops to which she brought us and helped with the purchase of Irish-made specialties.'[10]

In her late twenties when she met Jane Wilde in Dublin, Lotten von Kræmer was a leading feminist, who had endowed

---

8. Ibid., p. 87.
9. Lotten von Kræmer, *Samlade Skrifter* (Stockholm: Samfundet de Nio, 1918), p. 14.
10. Cited in Karen Tipper, 'Lotten Von Kræmer's Visit to the Wildes' Dublin Home in 1857', *The Wildean*, No. 34 (2009), pp. 41–49.

a scholarship for women at Uppsala University and held weekly literary salons for all the leading philosophers and writers of the city. Through this close friendship, Jane Wilde was introduced to Rosalie Olivecrona (1823–1898), another leading feminist based in Stockholm and editor of a journal for Swedish women. Getting to know these two women, reading and commenting on the magazines that they ran, was a meeting of intellectual minds.

Jane Wilde's admiration both for these women and for a more enlightened society in Sweden is made clear in this account of her time in Stockholm, published some year later:

> Women take a very leading position in Swedish society. They are good linguists, well read and converse with grace and decision, as if their opinion were of some importance in a discussion. Intellect, good sense and graceful dignity are their characteristics, not coquetry or love of vain display. Many of them are writers, Madame Olivecrona, wife of the chief justice of Stockholm, was editor of a journal. She writes in English, French and German with perfect fluency and as much ease as in Swedish.[11]

After the initial meeting in Dublin, a lively correspondence began, with Jane Wilde often writing in Swedish after she had acquired some fluency. Lotten was introducing her to many contemporary Swedish women writers and was opening up her interest in Swedish history and folklore. Then in autumn 1858 Jane Wilde travelled with William via Hamburg, to Denmark, Norway and Sweden. There she was entertained by Lotten and her father at the governor's residence in Uppsala and began notes for her travel book on Scandinavia and also on Swedish folklore. She had been reading the novels of Swedish writer, Emelie Flygare-Carlen (1807–92) and had been teaching herself Danish and Swedish

---

11. Jane Wilde, *Driftwood*, pp. 195–196.

and translating poems from each language. By March 1862, she was writing to Lotten in Swedish. The Wildes returned to Sweden in August of 1859 and travelled onwards to Germany, where they visited the collections and museums in Berlin. This was to help her greatly with her own folklore collecting and provided her with an international context for her own writings on Irish folk traditions and superstitions.

Rosalie Olivecrona came to Dublin in August of 1861 to attend a conference for the British Association for the Promotion of Social Science. William Wilde had embarked on his extensive catalogue of Irish Antiquities for the Royal Irish Academy and the conference dealt with such valuable rescue work of historical and literary heritage in other countries. Jane Wilde was very much part of this conference and may have attend the trip organised to the Aran Islands for all the delegates. During the conference, the Swedish delegation had open house in Merrion Square. The Wildes travelled back to Sweden in October 1861, for William Wilde to receive the Order of the North Star from the King of Sweden. Jane Wilde was anxious to improve on her own Swedish and asked her friends if they could find her a governess who could also speak French and German. Also, a poem of Jane Wilde's from 1847, called 'Man's Mission' was translated and published in Sweden. She wrote to thank Lotten: 'I really felt something of the exaltation of fame when I opened the Swedish and found Man's Mission' translated into your musical language. Are you the fairy magician?'[12]

It was her Swedish friends who encouraged her to start her own Saturday afternoon literary salon in Merrion Square. They had been hosting similar events in Uppsala and Stockholm and so Jane Wilde began to invite writers and artists to Merrion Square, always on Saturdays They soon became popular, and writers like Rosa Mulholland were regulars and spoke of her welcoming kindness. Catherine Jane Hamilton has left an account of her first time in

---

12. Fitzsimons, p. 32.

Number One, Merrion Square and of the gracious and welcoming social skills of Jane Wilde:

> Though I was a perfect stranger to her, she at once made me welcome, and introduced me to someone she thought I would like to know. If anyone was discovered sitting in a corner unnoticed, Lady Wilde was sure to bring someone to be introduced and she never failed to speak a few happy words, which made the stranger feel at home, As to her own talk, it was remarkably original sometime daring and always interesting. Her talent for talk was infectious, everyone talked their best. There was tea in the back room but no one seemed to care about eating or drinking.[13]

There was some disapproval of the bohemianism of the visitors but the *Irish Times* of 11th March 1878 commended the fact that 'The charm in the society to be met in Lady Wilde's salons was that it was wholly devoid of that species of snobbishness generally so fatal to social gathering in Ireland. Talent was always considered by Speranza a sufficient recommendation to her hospitality.' On the other hand, *The Athenaeum* was worried that she gathered to her soirées those 'whom prudish Dublin had hitherto kept carefully apart.'[14]

Many distinguished scientists, writers and leading feminist activists were invited to speak at Merrion Square, and music was always a feature. Nineteenth-century feminist politics and the struggle for the civil and legal rights of women was a strong connection between Jane Wilde and her Swedish friends. At one point, Jane Wilde wrote to them about Millicent Fawcett's visit to Dublin in April 1870, where the provost of Trinity College, and

---

13. C.J. Hamilton, *Notable Irishwomen* (Dublin: Sealy, Bryers and Walker, 1904), p. 186.
14. Fitzsimons, p. 34.

William Wilde and Jane Wilde herself spoke from the platform.[15] Her friendship with these two Swedish feminists led Jane Wilde to learn their language and to explore their myths and legends. She admired the work they did to enable women's education and at one point she wrote to them to say, 'Sweden ought really to settle handsome pensions on you both for having raised the character of your nation.'[16] The admiration was mutual and Lotten wrote about Jane Wilde in her own newspaper, commenting that

> Looking at her, the thought comes involuntary to mind that this is how the Roman matron must have looked at one time, with her classical pure features and with a Junoesque figure and bearing. But here the peace of the antient has made room for a mixture of soulful and attractive liveliness in her temperament. The fire in her gaze betrays the famous poetess whose lofty songs are so beloved in her homeland.[17]

Driftwood from Scandinavia (1884)

Eventually published in 1884, this is Jane Wilde's most substantial travel writing and draws on her trips to Scandinavia and Germany in the late 1850s and early 1860s. Her writings on her various trips to Sweden and to Scandinavia reflect the confidence of her views on a wide variety of disciplines, from poetry to ethnology and political life. Her persona as a travel writer is an attractive one, witty, appreciative, shrewd and always accessible in terms of writing style. Travel writing was itself a radical act of self-assertion for a woman writer, a way of taking control of the surveying and of a country and using the agency of the first-person narration to

---

15. Millicent Fawcett (1847–1929) was the founder of the National Union of Women's Suffrage Societies and was to co-found Newnham College in Cambridge for women.
16. Melville, p. 69.
17. Ibid., p. 71.

be the voice of assessment for Denmark, Norway, Sweden and Germany. Although William Wilde was her travelling companion on all her journeys to Scandinavia, she is the sole narrator, as if she were a solitary traveller, encountering each new culture with enthusiasm and wishing to find out as much as she could about the cultural life of each place. As with many nineteenth-century writers, she discusses the national character of each country in a collective sense, making general statements about the Celt or the Teutonic type. As an upper-middle-class writer who had written about the sufferings of her fellow Irish women and men during the Famine, she is always assessing the working people of each country to comment on the appearance of health and of national character as she could discern it. Michael Cronin points out that:

> In an essay entitled, "The Bondage of Women" Jane Wilde inveighs against the social and economic subjugation of women [...]. Above all, her view of patriarchy is that it fears more than anything else, the mobility of women, this dangerous, illicit, unchaperoned wandering from their assigned place in the social and economic order. Some women chose to break these fetters by engaging in the physical act of travelling and Jane Wilde does indeed produce her own travel account in 1884 entitled *Driftwood from Scandinavia*.[18]

She views each of these countries in light of her own interests in Irish cultural nationalism and always draws comparisons with the tyrannies of other counties with the iniquities of the British crown.

Structured around a leisurely progress from Dublin to Stockholm and then back home via Germany, the account opens by stressing the ancient links between Ireland and Denmark and the history of the Viking invasions and the fact that Dublin Castle was originally a Danish fortress. The ancient antipathy between the two nations

---

18. Michael Cronin, 'Lady Jane "Speranza" Wilde and the Translator's Invisibility,' *Claritas*, 8, 2002, pp. 83–102.

is her opening there, and she draws a contemporary note when she recounts the visit of the Princess of Wales, Alexandra of Denmark, to Ireland in 1866 and the murmurings against her. Jane Wilde always had an ambivalent attitude towards the women of the British royal family. In all her political writings she was vehemently opposed to the British regime in Ireland but, in some of her essays, she personally admired members of the royal family: 'Why should a Dane venture to come amongst them, a descendant of the ancient enemies of their race. But this last flicker of popular prejudice soon died out in the presence of the young princess. Her grace and charm at once won all hearts.'[19] This interest in the women of the British royal family is a constant theme of her travel book, with an account of the tragic fate of Queen Caroline Matilda of Denmark and many admiring comments on the Prussian Crown Princess, eldest daughter of Queen Victoria and her circle of writers and intellectuals in Berlin. There may have been other reasons for this apparent contradiction. She was aware that many of her readers admired various royal public figures. Queen Victoria was very popular and would attract a wide readership, as would her eldest daughter. Also, Jane Wilde was interested in the public role of women, and always comfortable with being well known and discussed herself and so there was a feminist interest in the areas in which women's behaviour and influence in public life would be most apparent; royal women had always been visible and often scrutinised. Her poetic skills and her interest in translation are also to the fore in this book, where she includes her own translations of many of the most popular poems from each country. Her gaze is never an imperial or occupying one but she reads each landscape and each set of peoples considering the assumptions around race and national character that were prevalent in the nineteenth century. Jane Wilde laments the lack of any Danish residents in Dublin, where she tried to find a teacher to help her acquire

---

19. Jane Wilde, *Driftwood*, p. 9.

the language. She was forced to try and teach herself and when she did finally arrive in Copenhagen, found that her words were incomprehensible to the people she met. She decries the lack of any real connection between Dublin and Copenhagen in the mid nineteenth century.

Always her commentary is entertaining and full of wry observations; travelling overland via Yorkshire, she takes time to claim the Brönte sisters as Irish and weird. On the boat from Hull to Hamburg, she lists the fellow passengers as 'A handsome Hamburg family, several Hull merchants, an alligator, a hyena, six Germans and six monkeys, all bound for Germany.'[20] She describes reindeer sandwiches as suggesting too forcibly sliced boot and she remarks that the silver saltcellars in her hotel dining room in Copenhagen may have been at the memorable wedding breakfast of Hamlet's mother, so antique did they look. It is interesting to note that she visited the synagogue in Hamburg. In Copenhagen, she visits the museums and recounts the tale of the English Princess, Caroline Matilda, queen of Denmark, who was imprisoned for adultery and died young and whom Jane Wilde constructs a kind of democratic rebel against the totalitarianism of the Danish royal family. She includes her own translation of the poem 'The Mystic Tree' by the Danish Romantic poet, Adam Oehlenschläger, (1799–1850) and shows her familiarity with contemporary Danish art and letters. She discusses the achievements of Hans Christian Andersen (1805–1875) and the artist Bertel Thorvaldsen, (1770–1840). This artist spent most of his career in Rome and she visited his gallery and admired greatly his influence on the Copenhagen style of architecture and of public buildings.

Her own intellectual interests found rich inspiration in Copenhagen and her respect for the care and cultivation of art and the preservation of antiquities struck a chord with her own concern about the loss of native Irish art forms. She was attracted

---

20. Jane Wilde, *Driftwood*, p. 16.

to Danish poetry and found much that echoed her own aesthetic interests, particularly in the ballad form. She remarked that 'Denmark is peculiarly rich in ballad literature, both legendary and historical, and in all in these simple metrical narrations all harshness of the language seems to dip away and leave only a soft music fit for the lips of childhood.'[21] This is her own version of the Undine legend, with no clear evidence of an original source:

> Undiné by the lonely shore,
> In lonely grief, is pacing;
> The vows her perjured lover swore
> No more with hope retracing.
> Yet none in beauty could compare
> With ocean's bright-haired daughter.
> Her cheek is like the lotus fair
> That lieth on the water;
>
> Her eye is like the azure sky,
> The azure deep reflecteth;
> Her smile, the glittering lights on high,
> The glittering wave collecteth.
> Her robe of green with many a gem
> And pearl of ocean shineth,
> And round her brow a diadem
> Of rosy coral twineth.

The Undine myth attracted her interest, the beautiful gentle sea nymph who had no soul and could only gain possession of one by union with a mortal. Jane Wilde spends some time in her travel book ruminating on the differences between men and women and wonders if such a myth gestures towards the gendered notion that 'Woman always loves heavenward; she has the instinct of ascension

---

21. Ibid., p. 91.

like flame and ether. Man, always loves earthward; he gravitates to earth, not to spirit; so that we may formulate; thus Love always gives soul to a woman, but takes it from a man.'[22] Her concept of marriage as profoundly differing for men and for women is a striking one and one that surfaces in her other writings. Jane Wilde concludes her rumination on the Undine myth and on her translation with the ambiguous warning, 'Let all genius remain unwed.'[23] Lest there be any ambiguity, Jane Wilde makes it clear that the risk to men of genius in making the wrong marriage is much greater than the risk to women. In a sense, domestically minded women are enemy to creative freedom. This attitude jars with her friendship with her Swedish friends, leading feminists in their own country, and her connections with other women writers, and yet her writings carry this contradictory impulse throughout her working life.

In her travelogue she spends a great deal of time describing the holdings at the great museum of antiquities at Copenhagen, the links with Irish art and the gold and silver holdings. She makes the shrewd and somewhat pointed remark that the prosperous Danish, unlike the colonised Irish, had never been compelled by poverty and economic necessity to melt down their ancient artefacts for the relatively small value of the precious metals. She notes the wealth of Celtic swords and weapons and praises the achievements of their civilisation, arguing for a kind of necessary reciprocity between the Celt and the Saxon: 'The Celt is the upheaving, expansive electric force that sets the ideas in motion, which move the world while the Teuton is the organising power that brings them into coherence and order.'[24] Her detailed interest in Danish methods of ethnography informed her later publications and reflected her current interests and her observations around collection and preservation.

From Copenhagen, she moved on to Christiania and there

---

22. Ibid., p. 89.
23. Ibid., p. 92.
24. Ibid., p. 109.

gives a detailed description of the capital of Norway. In a direct commentary on the failure of British governance of the Kingdom of Ireland, she celebrates the self-reliance and the national pride of the Norwegians. Denmark had held sway until 1814 but Norway now was in union with the Swedish crown. Jane Wilde believed that the years since 1814 had reinvigorated Norwegian national selfhood, evidenced by the new university and the high esteem for the laws and literature of Old Norse: 'In all of these things, the Norwegians show their proud, free spirit.'[25] Jane Wilde saw Norway as being a much more egalitarian society, with a more equal distribution of wealth and a greater social equality. She celebrated this with a translation of a poem and song, 'For Norge', written by a Norwegian political figure, the bishop of Bergen, Johan Brun (1745–1816) in 1771. This song had been the rallying cry for young Norwegians against Danish rule and had been banned by the Danish authorities. Hearing it sung one evening, she made this English translation of what had become the Norwegian national song and a symbol of pride and identity:

> For Norway, Freedom's fatherland,
> Fill up the wine-cup flowing,
> And pledge it, brothers, hand in hand,
> To keep the hot blood glowing.
>
> By gyves and fetters rent we swear,
> No tyrant's hand shall ever dare
> To chain our souls, while swords we bear
> To guard old Norway's Freedom!

Her arrival in Stockholm provokes her to describe the various Scandinavian countries in terms of types: 'The Norse are democrats, the Swedes courtiers, the Danes artistic Bohemians.'[26]

---

25. Ibid., p. 131.
26. Ibid., p. 150.

And this is again, a constant intellectual preoccupation in her writings, the propensity to see countries as being inhabited by generically recognisable 'types.' Her visit to Sweden included time at the Viceroy's castle in Uppsala with her friend, Lotten: 'She has endowed a scholarship at Uppsala University for women and thus the mind and energies of the long-oppressed sex have received an immense stimulus to exertion.'[27] Nor does she forget her other friend: 'Madame Olivecrona has published a very interesting pamphlet on the present condition of women in Sweden, from which it appears that they are now almost on an equality with men as regards educational advantages.'[28]

In this section of *Driftwood*, she includes her translation of 'Thecla, A Swedish Saga':

> On the green sward Thekla's lying,
> Summer winds are round her sighing,
> At her feet the ocean plays;
> In that mirror idly gazing
> She beholds, with inward praising,
> Her own beauty in amaze.
> And with winds and waves attuning
> Her low voice, in soft communing
> Said: "If truly I'm so fair,
> Might the best in our Swedish land
> Die all for love of my white hand,
> Azure eyes and golden hair."
>
> And fair Thekla bent down gazing,
> Light her golden curls upraising
> From her bosom fair to see,
> Which, within the azure ocean,
> Glittered back hack in soft commotion,

---

27. Ibid., p. 186.
28. Ibid., p. 201.

Like a lotus tremblingly.
Saying soft, with pleasure trembling,
"If so fair is the resembling,
How much fairer I must be!
Rose-lipped shadow, smiling brightly,
Are we angels floating lightly
Through the azure air and sea?
"Oh! that beauty never faded,
That years passing never shaded
Youthful cheek with hues of age!
Oh! thou fairest crystal form,
Can we not time's hand disarm?

Her journey continues with a trip from Stockholm to Berlin and then homewards by Hanover. There is a real shift in tone when Jane Wilde comes to talk about the Prussians, a kind of wary admiration with undertones of dislike. It is hard not to see her sense of humour underpinning her solemn pronouncements:

> The Celt always resisted dominant empires and bondage to routine, according to the instinct of all passionate, impulsive natures; for individuality in a human soul, and distinct nationality in a people, must be cherished to produce the fruits of genius, otherwise life becomes the mere mechanical work of a machine, not the spiritual work of the spirit. The Teuton instinct of law and organization has now reached its extreme expression in the Prussian military empire; but the people submit very apathetically, according to their nature, to the iron hand of the autocrat, and console themselves with beer and philosophy – a dreamy philosophy, vague and colourless as their plains, no landmarks for the eye or the soul, only infinite monotony of sand-drift and grey mist, in which all enthusiasm seems to have died out or become unfashionable... The black eagle of Prussia floats above us

– the vulture, it should rather be called, as nothing escapes its talons nor the desolating swoop of its terrible wings – and German resounds on all sides. It seems quite easy to speak, after the obscurities of Danish; but we scarcely need to practise our lingual knowledge, for all the Prussian officers on board speak English perfectly. The captain is monosyllabic and stern and is quite insensible to flattery. How to reach the heart of a Prussian is as difficult a problem as to find the fourth dimension. They are a very intelligent people, but morose. They cannot help it; they are born so. Courtesy is the grace of the Gothic branch of the Teutons only. On the third day after leaving Sweden, that land of noble hears and noble manners, we reached Stettin. It was evening. A sea of light was around us; a roseate mist filled the atmosphere, through which soft cloud masses rose like the snow-peaks of an Alpine world, and every peak was flushed crimson in the last rays of the setting sun. Thus transfigured, even Germany looked beautiful.[29]

There is a sense of anti-climax leaving a beloved country like Sweden, with the kind of society she admires. Germany leaves her much more ambivalent, and she shows her sense of ironic detachment in her account of her time in Prussia. She is very dismissive as to what she sees as the general physical type of the Prussian, denoting a kind of generic racial dullness, contrasted with the beauty of the Swedish people and the Irish people. She is unimpressed by the flatness of the Brandenburg landscape on her journey into Berlin and takes the time to remind the reader of the relationship between landscape and character, as she sees it, and drawing an Irish parallel: 'The Celt is willing to die, perhaps uselessly for an idea, the Saxon labour and lives for gain.'[30] Again and again, she seeks to understand national type, temperament,

---

29. Ibid., p. 230.
30. Ibid., p. 235.

and culture in the light of environment and climate and sees a distinct relationship between landscape and the character of a nation. This would inform her own sense of a more inclusive Irish identity as transcending class or religious identity. This idea of an aesthetic of inclusivity was later to inspire the writers of the Celtic Revival at the end of the nineteenth century, where the Irish landscape provided the imaginative inspiration for a vision of a free and unified Irish cultural nationalism.

She sets aside her dislike of the Prussian people when she recounts their struggles against Napoleon. Here, she casts them in the light of patriots fighting against an imperialist oppressor and includes her translations of the poems of Herwegh, his 'The Knight's Pledge' and those of Theodor Körner, including his poem 'The Sword Song.' Carl Theodor Körner (1791–1813) was a poet and soldier. It was said that he composed 'The Sword Song' in a pause during an uprising against Napoleon and then return to the fray where he died, at twenty-one. In his early death, she again finds parallels to her own time, the sacrifices of the Young Irelanders and her own poetic career with *The Nation*. Körner had died in battle and she exults at this romantic death and sacrifice: 'For him whose genius had inspired a nation to vengeance, there was no quarter.'[31] Likewise, Queen Louise, the foe of Napoleon, is her heroine, a beautiful young woman who sacrificed her life for love of country.

Her time in Berlin included a visit to the opera, time spent in the museums and observing the collections and the methods of preservation. The Crown Princess, Victoria's daughter, earns warm approbation from Jane Wilde: 'She is the head and leader of intellect in Berlin.'[32] She must also have been aware of her London audience and thus wrote to the general interest in British royalty. She finished with a plea to the reader to travel to Germany and Scandinavia: 'Whoever desires fresh impulses, renewed vitality,

---

31. Ibid., p. 249.
32. Ibid., p. 272.

increased nerve power and to find the means of sending a new spring of life rushing up through the wearied heart, let them sail away to the beautiful islands of the Baltic, plunge into the glorious pine forests of Sweden.'[33]

In 1884, when *Driftwood from Scandinavia* was published, Jane Wilde received fifty guineas from the publisher, Richard Bentley and was promised a further fifty if another edition was published. Jane wrote in January 1885 to Lotten, to tell her that the book had pleased her publisher and also anxious to see if any reviews had appeared in Sweden, concerned that she has not heard from her Swedish friends for a long time: 'One trembles at a long blank silence and I have such a loving memory of Sweden. I ought not to be forgotten – dear Lotten.'[34]

After the travels described in *Driftwood in Scandinavia*, their social position in Ireland was further augmented when William Wilde was appointed Surgeon Oculist in Ordinary to the Queen in Ireland. Then, for his work on the Census Reports, he was knighted in January 1864 at Dublin Castle, with Jane Wilde now becoming Lady Jane Wilde and wearing her richest gown to the ceremony. In the summer of 1864, she wrote to Rosalie Olivecrona to complain happily that 'so many dinners and invitations followed on our receiving the title to congratulate that we lived in a whirl of dissipation. Now we are quiet and I begin to think of re-awaking my soul.'[35]

As part of his schedule of appointments in that year of his success and achievement, William gave a public lecture at the Metropolitan Hall in April 1864, on the subject of 'Ireland, Past and Present, the Land and the People.' This lecture, which was later published in pamphlet form, is worth considering here as it provides a real contrast to Jane Wilde's Famine poetry. William Wilde had worked as a general practitioner, at some personal risk,

---

33. Ibid., p. 284.
34. Karen Tipper, *The Wildean*, No. 34 (January 2009), pp. 41–49.
35. O'Sullivan, p. 56.

during the Famine years, to alleviate the worst of the typhoid epidemic that had raged throughout the countryside. Afterwards he conducted his survey of the various illnesses that had arisen because of the Famine. Therefore, his rather stark views on the medium-term economic consequences for the drastic loss of life reflect his scientific considerations:

> Let me now turn to the *present*... During that long period, which dates from the early occupation of Ireland by the Celtic race until now, Firbolgs, and Tuatha de Danann mixed with Milesians, have gradually but steadily pressed towards the setting sun, and finally accumulated in the south and west, there living for the last century at least upon potatoes and with a landholding scarcely capable of supporting human life, and paid for, not by its produce but with money continually earned in England or at public works at home, and continually crying for aid and not to be relieved from the consequences of food failure. Often magnified and sometimes unjustly denied, which though practical in extent, were almost perennial in occurrence, since the sudden potato blight, Famine, and mortality of 1745, until that cycle culminated in the great calamity through which we have so recently passed. Thousands of the race remains yet in Connaught and parts of Munster, although thinned out by the Famine, the pestilence and by emigration, eking out a miserable existence on one or two acres of land, and, as I have already stated, earning the price of it by annual harvest migration. Twenty-two years ago, there certainly were in Ireland about eight and a half million of people. Had the rate of increase continued at even the low calculation of one per cent, per annum, what, think you, would our population have been now? Upwards of ten million – a number that England, with all her wealth and manufactories, has occasionally found difficult to feed

in times past. What would have become of them, I know not; but this I do believe, that had not events to which I have glanced in a previous part of this lecture taken place, some of us would not have had as good dinners as we seem to have enjoyed today; few would have been able to wear as fine clothes; nor should I have been addressing as happy and smiling faces as I see around me.[36]

His assessment of the economic results of the Famine contrasts rather unattractively with Jane Wilde's impassioned sense of injustice and of compassionate grief at the catastrophe of the loss of life, illness, and widespread emigration. There is a kind of hard logic here that makes difficult reading.

As the audience gathered for the lecture, outside the hall, another drama was unfolding. A young woman called Mary Travers was staging a protest. Newspaper boys held up placards with the words 'William Wilde' and 'Speranza' in bold letters and offering for sale copies of William Wilde's letters to Mary Travers and a pamphlet called 'Florence Boyle Price or a Warning by Speranza.' This was not a publication by Jane Wilde but rather, was a forgery or a parody by Mary Travers, who was conducting a campaign of stalking and harassment against the Wildes. This campaign would soon have Jane Wilde in a courtroom again. This time, Jane Wilde gave her side of the story in the witness box. As with the trial of *The Nation*, her writing was also placed on trial and her public role as an Irish nationalist poet under interrogation.

The Mary Travers Trial

This episode in Jane Wilde's life was to bring her a great deal of public attention and was, in the long term, to dominate her literary afterlife. The trial itself became another moment where her public persona as 'Speranza' was central to the newspaper reporting. Her

---

36. Walshe, *Selected Writings of Speranza*, p. 99.

reputation as a writer and as a translator of potentially radical and subversive literature became part of the prosecution case against her. In many ways, the persona of Speranza was on trial during this time and Jane Wilde's own brilliance as a public performer, her wit and her dexterity in giving evidence and confounding the attacks of the prosecution won the day for her.

The case was for libel and Jane Wilde was sued by Mary Travers for a letter Jane had written to the young woman's father, Dr Robert Travers. In this letter, Jane Wilde warned Dr Travers that his daughter's behaviour was becoming increasingly deranged and that her reputation was being compromised. The letter, an incautious one, came after much provocation and was Jane Wilde's desperate attempt to keep Mary Travers away from her and her family. The subsequent trial gathered much prurient interest in Dublin due partly to the fact that Mary Travers may have been a lover of William Wilde's and that Jane Wilde was aware of this relationship.

Mary Travers had been a much younger friend of the family for many years, a welcome guest in Merrion Square but, in recent years, this relationship had gone badly wrong. William Wilde had begun treating Mary in 1854 for a problem she had with her ear and gradually she had become his companion at many events, joining him and Jane Wilde at the inaugural meeting of the British Association for the Advancement of Science in Dublin in 1859. William Wilde had given her money, employing her as an assistant on his cataloguing for the Royal Irish Academy. Mary Travers seems to have had an equally close friendship with Jane Wilde, accompanying on her carriage journeys with her children around Dublin and visiting her in Merrion Square. For reasons that are not at all clear, the relationship had soured in recent years. Both Jane and William Wilde had backed away from her, although she joined them for Christmas dinner in Merrion Square in 1861.

William had paid for her to go to Australia in 1862 but she never made the journey and returned to Dublin to find her friendship with the Wildes becoming more and more fraught. At one point, Jane Wilde left her waiting downstairs in Merrion Square for several hours. The furious young woman took to persecuting them. Mary Travers took an overdose of laudanum in William's surgery and then put garlic in the soap dishes provided for his patients. She announced her own death in the newspaper in July 1863. Jane was as much the object of the anger of this young woman as William and the writing of her pamphlet 'Florence Boyle Price' was Travers' next attack. In this, published under the name of Speranza, Mary Travers implied that she had been drugged and assaulted by William Wilde. This pamphlet was then printed in a run of one thousand copies and widely distributed, dropped into letterboxes of houses all over Dublin. William Wilde was here represented under the name of Dr Quilp, after the villain of the Dickens novel, *The Old Curiosity Shop*. The pen picture of Jane Wilde as Mrs Quilp was hostile but unmistakable: 'Mrs Quilp was an odd sort of undomestic woman. She spent the greater portion of her life in bed and except on state occasions, she was never visible to visitors. Therefore, when she gave an entertainment, it was perfectly understood by her circle that a card, left by her guests on the hall table, was all she required of those who had enjoyed her hospitality.'[37]

Mary Travers seemed particularly incensed at her snubbing at the hands of Jane Wilde and her anger took the form of a particular obsession with her public persona as Speranza. Later Jane Wilde was to write to a friend and remark that 'Nothing made her so furious as my literary reputation.'[38] Travers wrote poems for *The Dublin Weekly Advertiser* under the name of Speranza and published another poem, full of venom and referring to William Wilde's other children:

---

37. *The Freeman's Journal*, 14th December 1864.
38. Melville, p. 105.

> 'Your progeny is quite a pest
> to those who hate such critters
> Some sport I'll have, or I'm blest
> I'll fry *the Wilde breed in the West.*
> When you call them *fritters*
> The names are not equivocal,
> They dare not by their mother's call
> Nor by their father, tho' he's a sir
> A gouty Knight, a mangy cur.[39]

Under this provocation, Jane Wilde left Merrion Square for Bray but Mary Travers followed her there, sending a boy into her house there to display a placard. Finally, on 6th May 1864, as a last resort, Jane Wilde wrote this letter to Robert Travers, a scholar and assistant keeper of manuscripts at Marsh's Library in Dublin. It was an attempt to put an end to the campaign of harassment.

> Sir – You may not be aware of the disreputable conduct of your daughter at Bray, where she consorts with all the low newsboys in the place, employing them to disseminate offensive placards in which she makes it appear that she has had an intrigue with Sir William Wilde. If she chooses to disgrace herself that is not my affair; but as her object in insulting me is the hope of extorting money, for which she has several times applied to Sir William Wilde, with threats of more annoyance if not given. I think it right to inform you that no threat or additional insult shall ever extort money for her from our hands. The wages of disgrace she has so loosely treated for and demanded shall never be given.
>
> Jane F. Wilde

The letter was an outburst of anger from a tormented and angry

---
39. O'Sullivan, p. 124.

Jane Wilde, Mary Travers had been impersonating Jane Wilde, and it was a measure of public recognition of her as the writer Speranza, that such a usurpation could take place and that it could hurt her so much. The letter had no immediate effect as Robert Travers took no action to restrain his daughter. Instead, it led to the libel case. Mary Travers found this letter some weeks later when she broke into her father's writing desk and she took it to a Dublin solicitor to agree to act on her behalf. Jane Wilde was issued a writ by a Dublin solicitor for 2000 pounds in damages.

On the face of it, Mary Travers had a valid case to make against Jane Wilde for libel and the wise course would have been to pay up, but the Wildes decided to go to court rather than settle. Legally William Wilde was also implicated as, under Victorian law, a husband was responsible for any legal debts and fines incurred by a wife. On 12 December 1864, the case of Travers versus Wilde opened in the old Four Courts in Dublin, with crowds thronging to be admitted and all the newspapers covering each day of the trial. The wit and skill of Jane Wilde's public performance during the trial helped her to win popular and media approval as her literary reputation was at stake and her own writings used against her. Isaac Butt, who had been a friend of both the Wildes, was the prosecuting council and he made no allowances for this friendship in his attempt to make her admit that she knew and condoned an affair between her husband and Mary Travers. This Jane Wilde was too clever to do. Butt made much of the fact that William Wilde was absent from the court all during the trial — 'A cowardly plea by which he shelters himself behind his wife'[40] — indeed the whole proceedings focussed on the two women in the case. Then Butt read extracts from Jane Wilde's translation of *The First Temptation*, denouncing the book as immoral and implicating Jane Wilde in that immorality as translator. Jane Wilde withstood his attempt to discredit her and won the sympathy of the newspapers by the wit

---

40. O'Sullivan, p. 130.

and the dexterity of her testimony. Being a public figure as a woman was a difficult position to navigate, especially when she might have known of her husband's relationship, but, by the end of the trial, all sympathy was on Jane Wilde's side. Emer O'Sullivan has written: 'In tales of passion, the betrayed wife typically elicits the spectator's sympathy. But Jane rebuffed the gallery's sympathy.'[41] (For example, Mary Travers had placed a notice in a newspaper making the false announcement that she herself had died, and when Jane Wilde was questioned as to when some meeting had taken place, she replied that it was in the August after Travers' death.)

Mary Travers found her reputation completely undermined and her addiction to opium hinted at. After the verdict, when Mary Travers was awarded a farthing for her honour, William Wilde was forced to pay 2000 pounds in costs. All of the newspapers spoke up in Jane's defence. The medical profession took up William Wilde's side and *The Lancet* devoted a full editorial to the court case and said 'Of Lady Wilde, no one can speak except with sympathy and respect.'[42] *The Times* in London agreed: 'To English eyes, Lady Wilde's lot will appear to be the hardest for she had been subjected to annoyance which it was almost impossible to endure.'[43] Mary Travers, on the other hand, was almost universally attacked and damaged herself in bringing such a case and courting the glare of publicity.

The Travers libel case attracted widespread public interest and amusement as the private life and letters of the Wildes became public property.[44] Jane was the victor in terms of the sympathy of the press and Mary Travers became the easy target of salacious rumour and ridicule. Jane Wilde had no difficulty in discussing the case or even, in sharing the newspaper reports with her friends. In a letter to Rosalie Olivecrona, she wrote on January 1st, 1865:

---

41. O'Sullivan, p. 129.
42. Melville, p. 103.
43. *The Times* 20th December, 1864.
44. See my novel, *The Diary of Mary Travers* (Bantry: Somerville Press, 2014).

You, of course know by now of the disagreeable law affair in which we have been involved, I send you a few extracts from the various papers. The simple solution to the affair is this – this Miss Travers is half mad. All her family are mad too. She was very destitute and haunted our house to borrow money and we were very kind to her as we pitied her. She took a dislike to me amounting to hatred – and to endeavour to ruin my peace of mind, commenced a series of anonymous attacks. Then she issued vile publications in the name of *Speranza* accusing my husband. All Dublin now calls on us to offer their sympathy and all the medical profession here and in London have sent letters expressing their entire disbelief. Sir William will not be injured by it and the best proof is professional hours were never so occupied as now. All is over and our enemy has been signally defeated in her efforts to injure us.[45]

After this case concluded, and after the glare of publicity retreated, Mary Travers then spent the rest of her life in obscurity and had no further contact with the Wilde family, outliving them all, dying in 1918.

A grievous loss to Jane and William Wilde and their sons was the sudden death of the beloved youngest child, nine-year-old Isola in February 1867. She writes of the heart-breaking sudden death to her Swedish friend, who had met Isola and had been a favourite of the child's:

Dearest Lotten,

I write to you in deep affliction. You will see by the paper I send that we have lost our darling only daughter. She had been a little ill with fever in the winter, but recovered, then we

---

45. Karen Tipper, *Lady Wilde's Letters to Constance Wilde* (New York: Edwin Millen, 2013), p. 49.

sent her for a change of air to her uncle's – about fifty miles away – there she had a relapse and a sudden effusion on the brain. We were summoned by telegraph and only arrived to see her die – such sorrows are hard to bear. My heart seems broken – still I must live for my sons – and thank God – they are as fine a pair of boys as one would desire. But Isola was the radiant angel of our home – and so bright and strong and joyous. We never dreamed the word death was meant for her. Yet I had an uncontrollable sadness over me all last winter – a foreboding of evil and I even delayed writing to you till I felt in my heart more of energy and life – Alas! I was then entering into the shadow which now will never more be lifted.[46]

Lotten sent her sympathies and arranged for the obituary notice to appear in the Swedish newspapers. The family went into mourning and, to console her sons, Jane Wilde brought them to Paris in November but she herself resolved not to go into society for some time, in mourning for her beloved daughter.

Her writing life in Dublin continued with a poem published in 1869 on the death for her friend, the writer, William Carleton. Carleton, a controversial figure, had been born into a poor Catholic family in 1794 but had later converted to Protestantism and had campaigned against Catholic Emancipation. His work, particularly his 1830 collection *Traits and Stories of the Irish Peasantry*, had offended many with his criticisms of the Irish character but he had been a friend and correspondent of Jane Wilde from her early days of writing for *The Nation*. He admired her work, calling her 'The most extraordinary prodigy of a female that this country or perhaps any other had ever produced.'[47] Jane Wilde, in her turn, admired him and tried to keep him from despair at his failing literary reputation. She appreciated the value

---

46. Tipper, *Lady Jane Wilde's Letters to Fröken Lotten von Kræmer* (Mellen Lampeter: 2008), p. 45.
47. Fitzsimons, p. 28.

of his writings and saw a link between their literary ambitions, the wish to tell the story of the lives of ordinary Irish people. In 1848, responding to his gloom and depression at his lack of achievements, she wrote to him to encourage and cajole him into better spirits: 'It is distressing in the extreme to see a mind like yours deliberately killing itself by conjuring up imaginary gloom. [...] Let St Speranza, if you admit my canonization, work the miracle of your restoration.'[48] When he died in 1869, in Dublin, an unhappy and bitter man, she wrote this poem in his honour:

> Our land has lost a glory! Never more,
> Tho' years roll on, can Ireland hope to see
> Another Carleton, cradled in the lore
> Of our loved Country's rich humanity.
> The weird traditions, the old, plaintive strain,
> The murmured legends of a vengeful past,
> When a down-trodden people strove in vain
> To rend the fetters centuries made fast;
> These, with the song and dance and tender tale,
> Linked to our ancient music, have swept on
> And died in far-off echoes, like the wail
> Of Israel's broken Harps in Babylon.
> No hand like his can wake them now, for he
> Sprang from amidst the people: bathed his soul
> In their strong passions, stormy as the sea,
> And wild as skies before the thunder-roll.
> Yet, was he gentle; with divinest art
> And tears that shook his nature over much,
> He struck the key-note of a people's heart,
> And all the nations answered to his touch,
> Even as he swayed them, giving smiles for gloom,
> And childlike tenderness for hate that kills –

---

48. Tipper, *Lady Jane Wilde's Letters to Constance Wilde*, p. 97.

As rain clouds threat'ning with a weight of doom
Flash sudden, silver light upon the hills.
But, he had faults – men said. Oh, fling them back
These cold deductions, marring praise with blame;
When earthquakes rend the rocks they leave a track
For central fires issuing forth in flame;
And by the passionate heat of gifted minds
The rudest stones are crystallised to gems
Of glorious worth, such as a poet binds
Upon his brow, right royal diadems
Like the great image of the Monarch's dream,
Genius lifts up on high the head of gold,
And cleaves with iron limbs Time's mighty stream,
Tho' all too deep the feet may press earth's mould.
Yet, by his gifts made dedicate to God
In noblest teachings of each gentle grace
Through every land that Irishmen have trod
We claim for him the homage of our race.
With pen of light he drew great pictures when
Nothing but scorn was ours; and without fear
He flung them down before the face of men,
Saying, in words the whole world paused to hear:
So brave, so pure, so noble, grand, and true
Is this, our Irish People. Thus he gave
His fame to build our glory, and undo
The taunts of ages, – strong to life and save
So, with a nation's gratitude we vow
In every Irish heart a shrine shall be
To The Great Peasant, on whose deathless brow
Rests the star-crown of immortality.
The kings of mind, unlike the kings of earth,
Can bear their honours with them to illume
The grave's dark vault; so Carleton passes forth,
As through triumphal arches, to the tomb.

This poem was published in *The Nation* and reflected her warmth and admiration for him. His sense that he struck the keynote of a people's heart was also her own poetic ambition. She had been patient with the unhappy and difficult man, writing to her friend John Hilson who had expressed his reservations about the older poet's intemperate language: 'You have misjudged my friend, Carleton or judged too literally. One must not paraphrase a Poet into the prose of everyday life [...] Carleton is one who it seems to me cannot help throwing the fire of his nature into every word. If he were colder, he would not be the genius he is.'[49] Jane Wilde empathised with Carleton's openness, his energy, his lack of restraint and caution, sharing some of those qualities herself. However, at one point in their friendship, she did have to ask the married Carleton 'to moderate his effusive language as it seemed to border on flattery, unworthy of both him and her.'[50]

Her interest in French politics and culture continued and in June 1871, she published a poem called 'The Vendôme Column' in *The Nation*, praising Napoleon III, 'Oh, not with the fall of the Column/Can perish his glory and fame.' Her relationship with the changing political landscape of Dublin was more complex and, to some extent Jane Wilde was beginning to find found herself now at a distance from contemporary Irish revolutionary politics. She had always been a nationalist and her distrust of armed republicanism was growing as time passed. Now as the occupier of one of the most prestigious addresses in Dublin, more anxious about the implications of revolution and disorder than when she had been a young woman, living with her mother in Leeson Street. As well as that, in the opinion of Emer O'Sullivan, 'It would be an historical error to identify the ideology of Fenianism and its descendants with that of Young Ireland and its support for cultural nationalism.'[51] In February and March 1867, there had been a Fenian rising organised

---

49. O'Sullivan, p. 58.
50. Tipper, p. 27.
51. O'Sullivan, p. 145.

by the Irish Republican Brotherhood and many of the leaders arrested. Jane Wilde was not in political sympathy with this latest version of Irish republicanism and had written to Lotten in the previous year to say, 'Heaven keep me from a Fenian Republic.'[52]

Jane Wilde's travels in Scandinavia and her interests in European poetry were all manifestations of part of her intellectual cosmopolitanism and in her writings, she used her learning to claim Ireland's ancient heritage as part of a greater European tradition and worthy of equal respect. She was unhappy with what she saw as the lack of pluralism and the insularity and thus with the failure of the younger generation of Irish Republicans. She wrote to Lotten von Kræmer in July of that year that, 'We are expecting a great uprising and revolution here. A great fear prevails but as we are both national favourites, I fear nothing personally – still times of sorrow trouble our lives.'[53] When the danger of revolution had passed, she expressed her relief but it is significant that when *The Nation* asked permission to reprint 'Jacta Alea Est', but this time under her name Lady Jane Wilde and she refused. Her growing sense of the need for cultural pluralism as the keystone to Irish cultural nationalism infused her writings, she was as committed as ever to Irish independence but was not in sympathy to the more violent measures being taken.

The Death of William Wilde and Aftermath

William Wilde's career continued to prosper. In 1873, the Royal Irish Academy awarded him the Cunningham Gold Medal. He began to spend more time in Moytura writing and researching and it was at this time that family finances began to disimprove, as his income from his medical practice reduced. In addition, his health was deteriorating and he gradually became an invalid, confined to bed while his wife took care of him during his last year

---

52. Tipper, *Letters to Lotten*, p. 43.
53. Ibid., p. 44.

of illness in Merrion Square. The strength and unconventionality of their relationship is clear from a memory from their son Oscar about a mysterious and regular visitor to his father' deathbed, who may have been the mother of Henry Wilson, present with Jane Wilde's approval.

In this time of uncertainty and grief, Jane Wilde turned to her poetry to reflect on her emotional and intellectual partnership with William Wilde and on the sense of loss she was experiencing as his death seemed more and more certain. In this poem, 'Related Souls', she remembers their shared dreams and the sense that their lives could last forever:

> All my soul's unfulfilled aspiration –
> Founts that flow from eternal streams –
> Awoke to life, like a new creation,
> In the paradise light of your glowing dreams,
> As gold refined in a threefold fire,
> As the Talith robe of the sainted dead,
> Were the pure, high aims of our hearts desire,
> The words we uttered, the thoughts half said.
> We spoke of the grave with a voice unmoved,
> Of love that could die as a thing disproved
> And we poured the rich wine
> And drank, at our pleasure,
> Of the higher life, without stint
> Or measure.[54]

This poem, understated, delicate and with a kind of moving melancholy was Jane Wilde's marking of the closeness in her marriage as their time together was ending, and a celebration of the ideas and the dreams they had shared. Likewise, in a three-page poem called 'The Soul's Question', published in the *Dublin*

54. Charles A. Read, ed., *The Cabinet of Irish Literature,* vol iv (London: Blackie and Son 1880), p. 83.

University Magazine in April 1876, she anticipates the loss of her beloved life partner. She wrote this poem at a particularly difficult period of her life, during the year of the last illness of her husband and at a time when she knew that he was dying. It was published within a few days of his death but she had found it impossible to write at all in the months before his death. Written in the form of a dialogue in which "the souls of the death-stricken" question Fate, she asks why they must suffer "this cruel, remorseless Death". There is a clear loss of conventional religious faith here, and no vision of a consoling afterlife:

> Can this be the end of all? The power of beauty and birth.
> The splendours of youth and brain, the laughter and songs of mirth –
> A nameless thing of horror to be hidden away in the earth?
> But as stones by the builders rejected, we are flung from the master's hand
> We – the makers and workers, the lords over sea and land.'

William Wilde died in Dublin, on 19th April 1876, aged 61, and was buried in Mount Jerome Cemetery with full honours, and a guard of representation from the Royal Irish Academy. His passing was marked with widespread tributes in the Irish and English newspapers and Jane Wilde wrote to one of his friends, 'I thank God that I was with him to the end and that the ministration of love and kindness was with him to the last hour.'[55] To Lotten she wrote, 'How my sad tears fell on the page of your beautiful and pathetic note so full of the truest, tenderest sympathy and feeling. I find now that all life to me is discord and every nerve thrills with dissonance and the future is ever so dark and uncertain. When the head of the house is taken, the whole edifice of one's life falls in ruins to the ground.'[56]

---
55. Letter to Sir Thomas Larcom, quoted in Melville, p. 129.
56. Tipper, *Letters to Lotten*, p. 58.

MERRION SQUARE (1851–1879)

Only after his death were the problems of their family finances now clear. As with many Victorian women of her class, Jane Wilde had little access or knowledge to her husband's financial affairs and her own finances were now precarious. He had left the house in Merrion Square to their eldest son, Willie, and the Bray houses to Oscar, but Willie's extravagant habits and lack of permanent employment meant that the money was not there to maintain the expenses of the household in Merrion Square for very long. Soon decisions had to be made about the future. Jane Wilde was dependant on the Moytura estate for her own income but these rents were infrequent and consequently she struggled to find a stable income for the rest of her life. Loyally, she made no complaint about William and concentrated on finishing his last book on Gabriel Beranger, including a glowing and tender tribute to his intellectual achievements when the book was finally published.

At the time of his death, William Wilde was working on a three-volume life of the antiquarian and illustrator, Gabriel Beranger. Beranger, a French Huguenot, was born in Rotterdam in 1729, and came to Dublin in 1750, keeping a print shop and sketching many ruins and relics around Ireland, dying in 1817. William began to collect his prints and volumes of his sketches of many now vanished churches and ruins. The first three sections of this book had already appeared in the Royal Historical and Archaeological Association of Ireland between 1870 and 1873 and then Jane Wilde wrote the fourth part for full publication in 1876. Here is William Wilde's own commentary on Beranger's achievements, an admiring account of his method of reclamation that tells us much of Jane Wilde's own processes of recovery in relation to Irish myths and folktales:

> Beranger, on the contrary, worked systematically at the art symbols of a people's life. He tracks their history in the savage gloom of the Druid's altar – the graceful form of the mystic pillar-tower – the fierce strength of the Norman fortress, and

the stately grandeur of the medieval abbeys and castles, with their splendour of architectural symmetry and beauty, and their sacred or warlike memories and associations. While our modern artists, for the most part, lavish their genius on the ever-changing moods of Nature, he gives us the changeless work of human minds – the passions and storms of great epochs – the warfare and the piety, the culture and the progress, of a people, as expressed and symbolised by their national monuments – in a word, the whole life of the past races out of which our nation was builder, and which only can be known by the works their hands have wrought, and the beauty of the ruins they have left. And it is, truly, a nobler thing for an artist to evolve the soul of a people from its monuments, and to give as subjects for our contemplation the steadfast historic landmarks of our country, than to note the atmospheric changes of our skies. Let us have both if we can, but not neglect the higher and greater aim while perfecting the lower.[57]

Steadfast historic landmarks also occurred in the folklore and the antiquities of the Irish past and these were to be the focus of much of Jane Wilde's writings in London. The completion of this book was a labour of love for Jane Wilde as the content reflected their shared wish that the important work of recording the rich legacy of Irish antiquities Beranger had initiated should be continued. It concluded with this very loving tribute to the character, the mind and the heart of William Wilde:

> It was the earnest wish of Sir William Wilde that Beranger's sketches, so rich in suggestions for our living artists, and so important to the antiquary and archaeologist, should be published in a volume along with the Journal. Probably more than two hundred of these interesting works of art may

---

57. Walshe, *Selected Writings of Speranza and William Wilde*, p. 119.

be still forthcoming. He would have undertaken the work himself, even at his own expense, had health and life been spared to him. But it is to be hoped that the project will not fall to the ground, and that the publication of so useful and valuable a book will be accomplished by someone with an intellect as energetic, a mind as well stored with the requisite knowledge, a heart as zealous for the advancement of Irish art and literature, as well the intellect, the mind, and the heart of Sir William Wilde.[58]

Never afraid of controversy, Jane Wilde continued to critique the British Establishment in Dublin. Although contemplating a move to London and in need of a pension from the British government, in 1878, she nevertheless published a pamphlet called *The American Irish,* where she railed against British rule in Ireland, praised the purifying power of suffering and the dire result of enforced emigration: 'All oppressed nations are eloquent. When laws forbid a people to arm, they can only speak or sing. Words become their weapons and the Irish armoury is always bright and burning.'[59] She reminded her readers of the ways in which Irish culture is popular in America and that the influence of American culture in Ireland and the Irish is to make them more interested in democracy and more intolerant of imperialism. America transforms the helpless Irish refugees, traumatised by Famine, into a proud independent people. Her anti-Englishness is notable here: 'Naturally the object of an alien government was to extinguish the idea of a country; to degrade and obliterate heroic memories; to brand a patriot as a traitor, and nationality as treason.'[60] She goes on to warn the British of the consequences of this forced emigration. With a large population of American Irish, keen to support any struggle for Irish independence, the British

---

58. Ibid., p. 119.
59. *The American Irish* (Dublin: William McGee, 1877), p. 2.
60. Ibid., p. 11.

were storing up trouble for the future and in this she was correct. She laments the stagnant nature of Irish society, impoverished by imperial neglect and indifference on the part of the British government: 'The present Prime Minister has never visited Ireland and knows so little of the country he governs.'[61] Her knowledge of the Irish-American press is impressive and she makes the point that 'A people who were learning, under the teaching of America, the dignity and value of human rights, are not likely to acquiesce tamely in the degraded position Ireland holds in Europe.'[62]

In 1880 the English writer, Alexandra Orr (1827–1903), an expert on Browning, wrote to her regarding this pamphlet, telling her that 'it is very eloquent and contains historical statements which are only too true but I cannot say that your estimate of the English character is just.'[63] Orr made the counter argument that the English were treating Ireland much better in the nineteenth century and that the American Irish would prove to be enemies to Ireland. Orr's view of Ireland was an imperialist one to say the least: 'And when you reminded us that we have destroyed the trade of Ireland as well as confiscated her soil, may we not remind you that we have taken these things for a people who, to use your own words, despise the one, and hate the toil without which the other is useless.'[64]

For the Wildes, finances continued to deteriorate in Merrion Square and Willie sold up his property in Dublin and left Ireland to take up the profession of journalism in London. With no income and no home, and, despite her vocal anti-Englishness at this period, Jane Wilde had no alternative but to follow him there and begin a new career as a free-lance writer.

---

61. Ibid., p. 35.
62. Ibid., p, 42.
63. Tipper, *Letters to Lotten*, p 138–9.
64. Ibid., p. 139.

CHAPTER FOUR

London (1879–1896)

Jane Wilde moved to London in May 1879, at the age of fifty-eight. The decision to leave her home in Merrion Square, where she had lived very happily for more than twenty years, was a difficult one. William Wilde had left her in a precarious financial position, and she was now dependant on her son Willie, who was incompetent in most practical matters and was to become dangerously insolvent and struggling with addiction. With characteristic energy and with a great deal of spirit, she succeeded in establishing herself in London and found that she could write to support herself. Her time in London was not simply a time for retirement and survival after the loss of her Dublin home and lifestyle. Rather it was to be a time of intense literary productivity for her, with the publication of four substantial books and collections, a great deal of reviewing and the establishment of another successful literary salon. Most of her important essays and her folklore editions came from this time in London, a significant revival for her career and for her literary reputation. This achievement was more impressive because of the financial uncertainty and instability in her domestic life. Her son Willie was of no assistance to her in money matters. Rather he became a drain on her resources and her health. In this section, her literary connections and publications from her time in London will be explored.

As soon as she arrived in London, she wrote to Oscar, always a source of assistance, to tell him of the very unpromising circumstances of her arrival: 'I know nothing of Willie's wishes. Is the furniture to be sold or brought over? I know not. I think I will die and end it. Meantime I have a dozen trunks and books to put somewhere. But where? Your deplorable mother, Senza Speranza. (Without hope).'¹ Soon she took matters into her own hands, found a place to live and turned to writing to survive in this expensive city.

Although some poems were published in her time in London, her writing was mainly in prose, a more lucrative source of income. Her explanation for this move to a new genre comes in a letter to the English writer, David James O'Donoghue (1866–1917). He had compiled the biographical dictionary, *The Poets of Ireland* (1892–93), and had written studies on Carleton and others. O'Donoghue was gathering information for his book and wanted to how what she was writing at that time. Jane Wilde made this very striking claim: 'I have recently devoted myself more to literature than to politics. Nationality was certainly the first awakener of any mental power of genius within me and the strongest sentiments of my intellectual life, but the present state of Irish affairs requires the strong guiding hand of men – there is no place for the more passionate aspirations of a woman's nature.'² It is difficult to know if she was being ironic or if in fact she did believe in the gendered capabilities of women and men. As I will discuss later in this section, some of her essays complicate her position as a champion of women's rights. In many ways, Jane Wilde embodied ambivalent and often contradictory views on women's creativity. Her writings often advocated the need for women's rights, but she also held the view that domesticity was the real threat for the artist, and the world of the domestic was often, for her, a female world. Like many Victorian writers, Jane Wilde was conflicted in her ideological stances.

She continued her interest in Irish politics, attending

---

1. Tipper, *Lady Jane Wilde's Letters to Oscar Wilde*, pp. 60–61.
2. Tipper, *Letters to Constance*, p. 112.

Westminster to hear the debates on Irish issues and expressing her great admiration for Charles Stewart Parnell, the leader of the Irish Parliamentary party. Her interest in women's rights continued, and she was a passionate advocate of the establishment of a university for women. In 1883, she praised the landmark passing of the Married Women's Property Act by the British parliament with an essay called 'A New Era in English and Irish Social life for the Gentlewoman,' where she referred to it as 'an important and remarkable epoch in the history of women.'[3] (Had it been passed earlier, it might have saved her own capital from being lost in the financial disaster of the Moytura estate).

At first Jane Wilde and her son Willie settled together in a rented apartment in Knightsbridge. Oscar began to introduce her to her literary friends and contacts while she slowly built up a new career as reviewer and essayist. This assiduous networking in literary London paid off and led to frequent articles published by various outlets, like the *St James Magazine,* the *Pall Mall Gazette, The Burlington Magazine,* which was a monthly publication, and a society magazine called *Queen.* She also wrote for a women's household journal *Lady's Pictorial* where she reviewed the 1880 novel, *Endymion,* by the former prime minister, Benjamin Disraeli (1804–1881). (Later this review was to be expanded into an essay on his work in *Men and Women and Books*). She was careful with the subjects she chooses to write on, telling her friend Catherine Hamilton, author of *Notable Irish Women,* 'I cannot write about such things as "Mrs Green looked well in black and Mrs Black looked well in green.'[4] When she did write about clothes and fashion, she made sure that she drew social and moral lessons and observations from the subject, believing in the necessity of rational dress for women. Her essays always drew on classical literature for reference points and were grounded in her wide literary and historical readings and study. Her reviewing was well

---

3. Melville, p. 254.
4. Fitzsimons, p. 67.

regarded in literary circles in London and, in turn, her own books got reviewed by the leading journals.

Her intellectual and linguistic interests also found new stimulation in the new friends she made in London when she became part of a German language group. Writing to her friend Rosalie Olivecrona from her house on Grosvenor Square in 1883, she tells her that

> London is a great focus of life and intellect. I have met all the celebrities, Ruskin, Browning, and Matthew Arnold and others but still I dislike London, the life is too ponderous and expensive and expense is troublesome now for since the troubles began in Ireland and I have been paid any rents and have received nothing for the last four years from the property in Mayo that should pay me two hundred pounds a year. Ireland is in a bad state. All the gentry were ruined and the shops are bankrupt.[5]

This was to be a constant worry for her. For example, in 1882, Oscar was sending her money to settle his own bills and he told her to keep the balance to cover her own debts. She wrote back, lamenting her own lack of income: 'It is dreadful taking your money. Destiny does such ill-natured things. Whenever one member of a family works hard and gets any money, immediately all the relations fling themselves on his shoulders.'[6] His success was a great delight to her and he always shared his good fortune with her, but when Willie managed to fall out with Oscar, it took all of her patience and care to try and effect a reconciliation between her two sons.

Jane Wilde had re-established her Saturday literary salon by 1882. Despite her limited financial circumstances and the modest lodgings she now occupied, many writers and public figures made

---

5. Tipper, *Letters to Constance*, p. 63.
6. Tipper, *Letters to Oscar Wilde*, p. 48.

their way there. Like her Dublin salon, it was a great success. Irish writers like her old friend from *The Nation,* Charles Gavan Duffy, now knighted, George Moore, Katharine Tynan (who described Jane Wilde with admiration as being like a 'Druid priestess'[7]), Yeats and Bernard Shaw all attended. Other visitors included famous figures like Eleanor Marx, (who later defended Oscar in a journal essay published in Russia) and the poet Robert Browning. From America came distinguished visitors like Oliver Wendell Holmes and Henry Ward Beecher. In her letters, she mentions the presence in June 1884 of the feminist activist, Margaret Mary Maye, (1857–1914), who went on to publish her book *Women's Suffrage* in 1885. Jane Wilde always had a wide audience in the US and, at the time of her salon, Yeats wrote fondly of his visits there to her gatherings on Saturdays for the American press, telling his readers that 'When one listened to her and remembers that Sir William Wilde was in his day a celebrated raconteur, one finds it no way wonderful that Oscar Wilde should be the most finished talker of our time.'[8] (That her wonderful mode of speaking was her own and not derived from her husband needs mentioning, but at least Yeats did suggest the power of her influence over her son and his artistry, an influence Oscar was always first to acknowledge.) Later, in the aftermath of Oscar's downfall, W.B. Yeats was to prove a loyal friend to her, gathering letters of support from other Irish writers and always clear to acknowledge his debt to her writings for his own Celtic poems and publications.

Another visitor was Anna, Countess de Brémont. Born Anna Dunphy in 1894 in Ohio, she was an American journalist and singer who was married to Emile-Leon de Brémont, a medical doctor working in New York. Following his death, she moved to London, became friendly with Constance Wilde and with her mother-in-law. Anna de Brémont eventually published a (mostly) warm and loving memoir called *Oscar Wilde and his Mother* in

---

7. O'Sullivan, p. 254.
8. W.B. Yeats, *Letters to the New Island* (Cambridge: Harvard 1934), p. 77.

1911, dying in 1922 and buried, by coincidence, near Jane Wilde in Kensal Green Cemetery. She wrote of Jane Wilde: 'Never before or since have I met a woman who was so absolutely sure of herself and of what she was. I felt an absorbing respect for her courage in being herself.'[9]

As part of this growing success within London literary circles, Jane Wilde was made an honorary member of the Irish Literary Society in 1894. Oscar married Constance Lloyd in 1884 and a close friendship started between mother-in-law and daughter-in-law, as seen in their surviving correspondence and the many literary events they attended together. They both supported women's voting rights and the cause of rational dress for women and spent a great deal of time together. Jane Wilde's London writing continued to prosper when she published three articles in the *Pall Mall Gazette* in 1888, 'The Story of St Patrick', 'Mayday in Ireland' and 'Whitsuntide in Ireland', all derived from the success of her significant collection of Irish folklore.

Ancient Legends, Mystic Charms, and Superstitions of Ireland (1887)

From this interest in Irish folklore came one of her most important works, an account of Irish legends carrying the subtitle, 'With Sketches of the Irish Past'. Published in two volumes in London by Ward and Downey in 1887, it was also published in North America by Ticknor and Co. in Boston in the same year and would remain a popular collection that earned a wide readership. It was an area that had long interested Jane Wilde, as can be seen from her accounts of ethnography and folk collecting in Scandinavia and on continental Europe. Many of the Irish scholars and intellectuals she had known in her Merrion Square days had also worked on

---

9. Anna De Brémont, *Oscar Wilde and His Mother, A Memoir* (London: Everett, 1914), p. 45.

Irish language and Irish antiquities. For many Irish readers, her account of the traditions of Irish folklore would become the best-loved collection of Irish folklore for over a century. She would also provide inspiration for subsequent Irish writers and an accessible resource of the valuable folklore heritage for cultural nationalists.

In both volumes, she presents a wide range of legends in a series of short essays or episodes, each of them on topics related to folk traditions and beliefs. To make it more enjoyable she always illustrates her themes with lively and accessible dramatised stories from the Irish rural working class. Her ear for popular speech is an accurate one and her tone much less scholarly than in her reviews and essays, seeing each tradition that she recounts as an opportunity to present a dramatic moment. To achieve her effect, Jane Wilde demonstrates her considerable powers for dramatic reshaping of the specific folk narrative into a tale of rural life. She sees them as, in her own phrase, 'coming from the national heart.'[10]

A question arises as to where exactly Jane Wilde found these stories and traditions. She lived all her life in Dublin but did spend time in the West of Ireland at her holiday home in Moytura. She would also have had access to the resources of the Royal Irish Academy in Dublin. However, these collections were written in London and there is no record of her returning to Dublin at any time after the sale of the house in Merrion Square. She does say that these stories were taken down by 'competent persons skilled in both languages', but doesn't name them.[11] If they had been collected by William Wilde, she would have named him, and her own linguistic skills do not seem to have included a knowledge of the Irish language. In any case, the accessibility, range and liveliness of these collections of folk legend and custom became key to her literary reputation.

In her preface, she stresses the direct link between mythology

---
10. Jane Wilde, *Ancient Legends*, p. 7.
11. Ibid., p. 7.

and the physical remains of ancient monuments in constructing any cultural history and is anxious to confront the condescension and prejudice that such folklore can encounter in so called civilised societies. Jane Wilde nails her intellectual colours to the mast when she asserts that 'much remains unsolved, even to the philosopher, of the mystic relation between the material and the spiritual world.'[12] Her stance is a potentially controversial one for her audience in Britain and in the US, as she sees the traditions behind Irish folklore as outside any rational explanation or scientific understanding. Her late Victorian readership would also have been a readership with preconceptions and prejudices towards what was seen a primitive and sometimes violent Irish national character. However, Jane Wilde's strategy pays off, in that she taps into the interests in spiritualism and the occult that were also a feature of late-Victorian intellectual life and gives her study a Celtic flavouring and a universalising aspect that made it attractive to her readers: 'The superstition of the Irish peasant is the instinctive belief in the existence of certain unseen agencies that influence all human life.'[13]

In her introduction, she explores the context of these folk legends in an eloquent and confident essay, and her starting point is that there is a unity in all world legends, arising from an original language. Thus, she sees the urgent task of the ethnographers to acknowledge and trace this primary moment of universality and see the links between all folk cultures. In part, her ideological desire is to undermine any discriminating idea of a cultural pecking order and to re-assert the proper place of Irish mythology within the hierarchy of European cultural studies: 'It is therefore, in Ireland that above all, that the nature and origin of the primitive races of Europe should be studied.'[14]

Her ideological aim is to claim a Mediterranean origin for Irish

---

12. Ibid., p. 5.
13. Ibid., p. 6.
14. Ibid., p. 6.

myth, rather than a Nordic one, and this despite her love and admiration for Scandinavia. For Jane Wilde, Iran is the place of origin for Irish myth and culture. The gradual evolution of pagan belief into aspects of Christian iconography was a seamless one in her view, where the Irish are a race particularly open to a belief in the irrational and the spiritual. Her ideological aim here is to locate Irish mythology with a pan-European or Greek tradition, rather than seeing any link with a Saxon or Nordic point of origin. For example, she introduces her first story with a side swipe against the relative thinness of the English folk tradition: 'The tales and legends told by the peasants in the Irish vernacular are much weirder and stranger and have more of the old-world colouring than the ordinary fairy tale narrated in English.'[15]

She opens the first volume of the *Ancient Legends* collection with 'The Horned Women,' a striking tale of a late-night attack on a rich woman by a sinister band of horned witches, who take over her house one night, intent on killing her and her children. The woman of the house protects her sleeping family by a series of strategies or tricks, aided by a silent voice showing her how to rid her threatened domestic world of these evil and malevolent spirit women. This is one of the best examples of her skill in reproducing the drama of the original folk narrative. Many of her stories turn on this idea of the woman as the centre of domestic security and control, fighting malevolent spirit forces:

> And first, to break their spells, she sprinkled the water in which she had washed her child's feet (the feet-water) outside the door on the threshold; secondly, she took the cake which the witches had made in her absence, of meal mixed with the blood drawn from the sleeping family. And she broke the cake in bits and placed a bit in the mouth of each sleeper, and they were restored; and she took the cloth they had

---

15. Ibid., p. 17.

woven and placed it half in and half out of the chest with the padlock; and lastly, she secured the door with a great crossbeam fastened in the jambs, so that they could not enter. And having done these things she waited. Not long were the witches in coming back, and they raged and called for vengeance. "Open! Open!" they screamed. "Open, feet-water!"

"I cannot," said the feet-water, "I am scattered on the ground and my path is down to the Lough."

"Open, open, wood and tree and beam!" they cried to the door. "I cannot," said the door, "for the beam is fixed in the jambs and I have no power to move." "Open, open, cake that we have made and mingled with blood," they cried again.

The Horned Women are routed and forced to abandon the house they have invaded. Later stories follow on this lively ballad-like format and use the same sense of dramatic energy and include 'The Stolen Bride,' 'Legends of the Western Island,' 'The Fairy Child', 'Legends of the Dead of the Western Island' and 'Evil Spells and Festivals', and she deals with such well known folk ideas and traditions as 'The Banshee 'and the existence of the Sidhe.

Her line throughout is that Ireland has a direct connection with ancient and mystic cultures, bypassing its colonial neighbour. There is also a kind of authorial distance from her subjects, as if she is writing about a country and a class that she is observing and the class positioning, as with many Victorian writers on folklore, is very much at a distance: 'The Irish show their Aryan descent by the same characteristics as the Fairy race, for they also love everything that is artistic – the fascinations of life, beauty of form, music, poetry song, splendour and noble pleasures.'[16] This is her constant theme, the superiority of the Irish folk tradition over those of other European countries. For example, in 'Marriage Rites', she argues that 'The Irish, however, have retained more of

---

16. Ibid., p. 279.

the ancient superstitions than any other European people, and hold to them with a reverential belief that cannot be shaken by any amount of modern philosophic teaching. They are also, perhaps, indebted to Egypt for the wonderful knowledge of the power of herbs, which has always characterised the Irish, both amongst the adepts and the peasants.'[17]

Her interest in the heroic women of the past can be seen in her account of the mythic Queen Maeve: 'Maeve the great queen of Connaught holds a distinguished place in Bardic legend. When she went to battle, it is said, she rode in an open car, accompanied by four chariots – one before, another behind, and one on each side, so that the golden assion on her head and her royal robes should not be defiled by the dust of the horse's feet or the form of the fiery steeds.'[18]

In Volume Two, a wide range of legends and superstitions is explored, from animals to the role of medical superstitions and charms and the powerful influence in Brehon society on the poets and bards. She then continues with an examination of the stories and legends associated with the mainly male Irish saints, but she does note the fact that the sole Irish female saint that she mentions, St Bridget, held equal rank with the Archbishop. She examines in greater detail the legends of the Sidhe and the role of fairy life and legend in Irish myth and folklore. At the conclusion of the second volume, she includes her own review of John Gilbert's 1859 *A History of the City of Dublin.* She knew Gilbert, who had been a member of the Royal Irish Academy during her time in Merrion Square. In this review essay, called 'Our Ancient Capital,' Jane Wilde, herself a Dubliner, makes the intriguing statement that 'The concentrated will of Dublin has always been in antagonism with the feelings of a large portion of the nation.'[19] Here she is consciously placing herself as someone out of sympathy with Dublin's role as

---
17. Ibid., p. 219.
18. Ibid., p. 265.
19. Ibid., p. 283.

centre of the British administration of Ireland. The second volume concludes with a reprint of William Wilde's essay on 'The Ancient Race of Ireland', an address he gave to the Anthropological Section of the British Association in Belfast in 1874.

Ancient Legends, Mystic Charms, and Superstitions of Ireland was one of her best regarded and most influential publications and was to be one of the primary sources for Irish legends for several generations and well into the twentieth century when Ireland became an independent country. It enabled much of the writings on Irish folk culture and many of the writers of the Celtic Revival found inspiration here. W.B. Yeats wrote of this collection that 'We have here the innermost heart of the Celts in the moments he has grown to love through the years of persecution when, cushioning himself about with dreams and hearing fairy-songs, in the twilight, he ponders on the soul and on the dead. Here is the Celt, only it is the Celt dreaming'.[20]

Jane Wilde's main purpose was to demonstrate the complexity, originality, and diversity of Irish folklore, with the political message implicit that Ireland had a viable imaginative identity, derived from a very particular way of thinking and imagining. The recovery of this hidden mythology was more proof that Ireland was more than ready to be responsible for its own government. Not every critic welcomed her critique of British rule in Ireland. The review in *The Athenaeum* decided that 'It is sad to think that all the years Lady Wilde has dwelt in London has taught her nothing but hatred.'[21] What this critic recognised was that she constructed the recovery of this lost folklore as an act of resistance against imperial assumptions around 'native' art forms.

Her publication of these folk collections brings up the interesting question as to her connections with her son Oscar's writings. Jane Wilde clearly influences her son in terms of his commitment to feminism, his sense of the seriousness of the artistic vocation and

---

20. Melville, p. 199.
21. Sullivan, p. 289.

also in terms of his sense of the need for self-presentation and self-fashioning. More directly, much of her work has also influenced the underlying structures of his writings. Although he rarely wrote directly about Ireland or Irish matters in his essays and even in his poetry, perhaps feeling his parents had covered that field very comprehensively, new critical readings of his novel, *Dorian Gray* and of stories like 'The Fisherman and his Soul' have located evidence of underlying myths and archetypes derived from Irish folklore. In her essay, 'Wilde and Orality,' Deirdre Toomey makes links between Wilde's narrative structures and the art informing his mother's folk-collecting: 'Oscar Wilde can be associated with those Protestant nationalists (Sir William Wilde, Lady Wilde, Douglas Hyde, Lady Gregory, Yeats, Synge) who, by linking themselves to a despised, indigenous, pre-literate culture with folk-tales and folk parables, re-identified with Ireland.'[22] Toomey goes on to make the explicit link when she tells of the fact that his mother's tale, 'The Priest's Soul' was an after-dinner tale for him in Paris and concludes that 'Some of the images of Irish folk tales affected Wilde's sensibility.'[23] Likewise, in his 2005 study *The Faiths of Oscar Wilde,* Jarlath Killeen painstakingly traces the direct links between her stories of Irish traditional burial customs and, for example Oscar's 1874 poem on the death of his sister Isola, 'Requiescat.' Furthermore, in his 2007 *The Fairy Tales of Oscar Wilde,* he examines the imagery in 'The Selfish Giant' and links it directly with the folk collecting of his mother: 'White blossoms fill the air at the end of the selfish giant and demonstrate the connection between Wilde's fairy tale imagination and the imagination of the people he knew in the West of Ireland. Again and again in their studies, Wilde's parents return to these fertility rites and beliefs.'[24] When Oscar became the editor for *The Lady's*

---

22. Jerusha McCormack, *Wilde the Irishman* (New Haven: Yale, 1998), p. 34.
23. Ibid., p. 34.
24. See Jarlath Killeen, *The Faiths of Oscar Wilde* (Hampshire: Palgrave, 2005) and *The Fairy Tales of Oscar Wilde* (London: Ashgate, 2007), p. 77.

World and changed to name to *The Woman's World* in January 1888, she was one of the contributors to the first edition and later contributed peasant tales and poetry.

Ancient Cures, Charms, and Usages of Ireland (1890)

This next collection was her continuation of the important work as a folklore collector and again, the result of her years of study and interest and her ideological belief in the innate uniqueness of her own literary heritage. Here she is treading a difficult line, seeking to praise the wisdom of ancient cures and charms and to affirm their wisdom and shrewdness with contemporary scientific approval, but she also risks the colonial trope of the primitive and superstitious peasantry, unfit for the demands and the rationality of modernity. The use of the word 'Cure' in the title is, for example, a potentially risky one, courting ridicule for superstitious country beliefs, yet she keeps the balance between folklore and rationality throughout the book.

Her focus here is on the relationship between science and custom and in the opening section, called 'The Irish Doctors,' Jane Wilde makes her pitch for the validity of past customs and cures:

> From the most ancient pagan times, the Irish doctors were renowned for their skill in the treatment of disease, and the professors of medicine held a high and influential position in the Druid order. They were allowed a distinguished place at the royal table, next to the nobles, and above the armourers, smiths, and workers in metals; they were also entitled to wear a special robe of honour when at the courts of the kings and were always attended by a large staff of pupils, who assisted the master in the diagnosis and treatment of disease, and the preparations necessary for the curative potions.[25]

---

25. Jane Wilde, *Ancient Cures*, p. 4.

Again and again, she supports the customs and usage of past Irish physicians with the sense that they used observation and rationality: 'The skill of the Irish physicians was based chiefly upon a profound knowledge of the healing nature and properties of herbs.'[26] Yet she also justifies the use of magic and charms as being potent in dealing with nerves and with psychological illness, seeing an innate wisdom in the use of so-called 'charms' to complete the cure, using imaginative powers to reassure the troubled mind of the patients. This at a time when Irish nationalists were campaigning for the cause of Home Rule, and where a discourse around the uncivilised nature of the 'Celtic' race would undermine the drive for political independence. Instead, Jane Wilde is providing a lively yet dignified account of 'primitive' culture, arguing for its intrinsic value, won by generations of experience and observation. Her political impulse in collecting and publishing such a collection is made explicit when she pauses to observe that 'Nothing good in a nation's life is ever lost. The people will never go back to the servile bondage of soul and spirit that held them enchained before the fetters were rent and the bonds broken by the genius and intellectual force of the men of '48.'[27]

Her respect for the considerable work of her late husband in tabulating the rich tradition of Irish folk medicine is evident when she reminds the reader in a section called 'Ancient Medical Manuscripts' that

> Numerous copies of these ancient writers were made by the learned doctors and freely distributed among the profession, so that many of the manuscripts can still be found in the chief libraries of Europe. They are written on vellum and are beautiful specimens of penmanship. A commentary in Irish was sometimes added, besides which, several translations into Irish of the chief medical works, whole and entire, are

---
26. Ibid., p. 7.
27. Ibid., p. 131.

in existence. In proof of the great and accurate knowledge of these Irish physicians, it is stated by Sir William Wilde, that when preparing "The Status of Disease from the Earliest Times," for the Irish census, he was able to tabulate seventy-five fatal diseases accurately described by the native doctors, with many that were not fatal; and he asserts that the Irish terms for the principal diseases were of far more appropriate significance than those at present employed in English, or derived from the Latin and Greek.'[28]

Autobiographical elements are to the fore in Jane Wilde's exploration of the mythology of Irish medicine and she evoke the mythical battle of Moytura (the name of their estate in the west of Ireland that was so disappointingly not supplying her with her income) to provide an account of healing and of medical force in ancient Irish history:

> At this great historic battle of Moytura, Dianacht, the chief physician of the Tuatha, had a bath of herbs prepared, at the rear of the army, of singular efficiency, into which the wounded were plunged, and from which they emerged healed and whole. During the fierce combat, Nuada, the King of the Tuatha, lost his hand; but it is recorded that Dianacht made for him a silver hand, fashioned with the most perfect mechanical and artistic skill; and henceforth the King was known as *Nuada Airgeat-lamh* (Nuad of the silver hand), and by this name he lives in history.[29]

Her care in providing some sense of the mythic Irish names is noteworthy and the liveliness of her story of the battle of Moytura is in no way deflated by the fact that it never took place. Skill in the sciences, the supposed talent and monopoly of the so-called

---

28. Ibid., p. 10.
29. Ibid., p. 9.

Saxon race, is what she wants to establish and to show the skills of the ancient Celts. She proceeds with an account of popular cures and charms for specific ailments like epilepsy, deafness, and rickets, all illustrated via an appropriate folk tale, beguiling the reader with a lively narrative. Madness and its cure are illustrated via the story of Davy Flynn from Roscommon, surely a story she would have gleaned in her times in Moytura.

She describes such familiar customs as the visitation of the Banshee at moments of imminent death, and, in her version, St Patrick is reconstructed as a poet and as something of a magician himself. Her range of usages and customs is impressive, with a full account of May Day customs, Whitsun and the rites around death and birth. A common strand in her collection is the constant vigilance of the women of the countryside against the plundering wiles of the fairies and their desire to steal away mortal children and impressionable young men. Her other interest is in preserving the lost tradition of ancient charms. She writes of them in this way:

> A few examples of these ancient cures and charms may be given to show their simple, half-religious character, so well calculated to impress a people like the Irish, of intense faith and a strong instinct for the mystic and the supernatural. For the Falling Sickness "By the wood of the Cross, by the Man that overcame death, be thou healed." These words are to be said in the left ear while the fit is on the patient, and he is to be signed three times with the sign of the Cross, in the name of God and the blessed Lord, when by virtue of the charm he will be cured.[30]

Her tone varies throughout this book, sometimes she uses an historical or scholarly style to delineate the folk lore, or sometimes

---

30. Ibid., p. 201.

adopts the voice of the storyteller and even has elements of Hiberno-English in the narrative that she creates to mimic the tradition she is evoking here.

Her familiarity with William Wilde's cataloguing of the gold and silver collections of the Royal Irish Academy informs her section on 'Ancient Irish Gold', where she tabulates the range and richness of this collection and links each legend around the most important symbolic pieces held in the National Museum of Ireland. She is very sharp in her reproof that until relatively recently, no laws forbidding the melting down of ancient treasures for the limited value of the metal was in force in Ireland, because of the lack of respect on the part of the British administration for the value of ancient Irish artefacts. This had just been remedied by a law passed in 1861. Throughout this book, Jane Wilde's anger at the neglect of Irish heritage, the danger of such customs being lost and the need for preservation is made explicitly political. As if to underscore her purpose, and her anti-imperialist stance in this study, she concludes her book with a reprint of her pamphlet on *The American Irish* and the Irish of today, a polemic against British rule, which found disfavour with some of her reviewers. There was a perception that this collection was lighter in substance, even though W. B. Yeats again praised it in a review. It was her belief was that Irish superstitions had a kind of integrity and a uniqueness because they came from a population untroubled by recent invasion. Her knowledge of Scandinavian literature and myths was such that she could trace where the Norse and Viking cultures had influenced Irish folklore. With this sense of a unique cultural heritage, it was her hope that Ireland could revive its political autonomy by teaching the world about its innate and completely self-sufficient intellectual, imaginative, and spiritual legacy. This had been her long-held tenet of faith. In an earlier essay called 'The Fairy Mythology of Ireland',[31] published in the

---

31. *Dublin University Magazine,* July 1877, p. 73.

Dublin University Magazine she wrote, 'They have shewn such remarkable powers of fascination that the invaders themselves became *Hibernicis ipsis Hiberniores*.'[32]

Her finances improved following success in her application for pension of one hundred pounds a year from the Royal Literary Fund in 1888. This may have been assisted by her reputation as a reviewer and as an essayist within London literary circles. With that element of financial security, she was able to move to Oakley Road in Chelsea in October 1888 where she was to spend much of the remainder of her life. However, the gradual decline of the fortunes of her elder son, Willie, was to unravel this precarious security. In 1890, Willie married Mrs Frank Leslie, a prominent American journalist. Born Miriam Florence Folline in New Orleans in 1836, she was a successful newspaper owner and publisher and was known as Mrs Frank Leslie, owner and editor of the magazine of her late husband, *Frank Leslie's Illustrated Newspaper*. Mrs Leslie had attended Jane Wilde's Saturday salon and they became friends, as she was just the kind of successful and competent professional woman she admired. Jane Wilde was to write of her in her essay, 'American Women': 'She owns and edits many journals and writes with bright vivacity on the social subjects of the day yet always evinces a high and good purpose; and, with her many gifts, her brilliant powers of conversation in all the leading tongues of Europe, her splendid residence and immense income, Mrs Frank Leslie may be considered the leader and head of the intellectual circles of New York.'[33]

When she married Willie Wilde, Mrs Leslie insisted on settling one hundred pounds a year on Jane Wilde to help with her support in London. This marriage ended badly, with Willie drinking heavily and failing to keep his journalistic work commitments. Mrs Leslie was forced to take legal steps to end the marriage. After the divorce, Willie returned to London in debt to the tune of

---
32. Ibid., p. 74.
33. Jane Wilde, *Social Studies* (London: Ward and Downey, 1893), p. 144.

two thousand pounds but, despite the precariousness of her own finances, Jane Wilde insisted on foregoing the allowance from Mrs Leslie and always spoke well of her in the years to come.

Notes on Men, Women, and Books (1891)

This volume demonstrates Jane Wilde's intellectual range in that she collected her reviews and essays, including on Tennyson, Richter, Lamartine, and Swift; the specialist knowledge on Spanish, German, French, and English literature is impressive and makes this a very substantial volume of essays. As can be seen, each essay required a first-hand knowledge of the writer involved, a sense of their historical and cultural moment and an insight into the technical requirements of poetry, the novel and drama. The range and depth of her European subjects is very striking here. The subject of her first essay was the German Romantic writer Jean Paul Richter (1763–1825) author of the best-selling *Hesperus* (1795), who had lived in Weimar and was much admired by Thomas Carlyle and others in England and Ireland. Jane Wilde's extensive and knowledgeable essay is an object lesson in the struggle of an artist to succeed. She traces Richter's early life, the poverty of his upbringing, the repeated early failure to secure publication for his novels, 'his transition from the every-day life of reality to the higher ideal life of poetry and imagination.'[34] The essay demonstrates her close familiarity with his novels, and her analysis of *The Flower, Fruit and Thorn Pieces,* his best-known work to English-language readers, is entertaining and contains the now-familiar observations about the hero's domesticated wife and her lack of empathy with his life of poetry and imagination:

> She was one of those commonplace women who can never be raised from the dull prose of life into a lyrical inspiration

---

34. Jane Wilde, *Men, Women and Books,* p. 11.

for whom the great mystic universe is nothing but a nursery or a ballroom – whose souls have but the circumstances of their thimbles. Yet is it not her fault. Few, indeed, among women are the hearts at once tender and sublime – who can sanctify and individuate the earthly marriage bond and raise to yet higher grades the souls to which they are bound.'[35]

At the end of Richter's novel, the commonplace wife is disposed of and a much more suitable woman companion is now the reward of the hero, a woman who is both domesticated but also spiritually viable. Jane Wilde concluded that Richter himself found such a life companion, Caroline Meyer, 'A gentle, loving, patient, although learned woman, who could read Plato in the original and make her own dresses.'[36] Her tone is hard to catch here. Is she being ironic? Often Jane Wilde makes this observation, mirroring Victorian perceptions that women seem to possess more earthy, less spiritualised natures, deriving from their biological destinies, and this seems to sit uneasily with her feminist convictions. It seems clear, to me at least, that when Jane Wilde makes these observations, she exempts herself from her general view that women lack the capacity for higher spiritual and aesthetic achievements, but nonetheless saw genius as a male preserve.

Her essay on 'The Girondins' is a review of a book by the much-admired writer and politician, Alphonse Lamartine (1790–1869), with whom she corresponded. It is infused with her passionate identification with his *L'Histoire Des Girondins* (1847): 'All the brilliant pathetic, terrible, and tragic scenes of that supreme moment of French history are pictured there with an intensity of dramatic force, a vivacity of colouring and a splendour of diction such as no other poet or prophet of humanity has ever surpassed in grandeur and gloom.'[37] The French Revolution and the various

---

35. Ibid., p. 11.
36. Ibid., p. 15.
37. Ibid., p. 28.

political figures had provided her with much inspiration in her own days as the nationalist poet of *The Nation* and Lamartine's book was a crucial one for her in her own creation of an aesthetic. She commends French women involving themselves in the political movements of the French Revolution and castigates her own country for excluding women from political life: 'French ladies are wiser, there they seize instinctively on this additional instrument of fascination, so neglected by our countrywomen.'[38] Jane Wilde quotes Lamartine's words on Madame de Staël, in ways that could be seen as a self-portrait: 'A man in energy, a woman in tenderness, who wrote like Rousseau and spoke like Mirabeau – whose life was a dream of genius, glory and love […] That devoted ambition of a woman of genius to become the inspirer, the hidden destiny of some great man.'[39]

The rest of her essay on Lamartine's study of the Girondins concerns itself with another prominent woman of the French revolutionary period, Manon Roland (1754–1793). This account of the life and tragic death of this writer and *salonnière* is also in many ways is a self-portrait, as Jane Wilde expresses the view that to Roland, 'her country became the object that filled the infinite necessity of love in her heart. She became the passion, the sentiment of the Revolution and radiated around her its heat and light. And is it not thus with all women of genius when their first destiny, Love, has been crushed forever.'[40] Jane Wilde vehemently disagrees with the idea that violence is necessary to make revolution happen, her point of departure from the activities of the Fenians: 'It is a fearful error to maintain that the regime of the guillotine gave liberty to France. On the contrary, it destroyed it.'[41] And she is consistent in her dislike of Bonaparte and her sense that he was never a true revolutionary. She ends her account

---

38. Ibid., p. 30.
39. Ibid., p. 29.
40. Ibid., p. 32.
41. Ibid., p. 38.

of the history of the Girondins with the clear assertion that the true spirit of transformation was lost and this was a fatal ending to the potential for freedom and change that the Revolution seemed to promise.

Later essays included a lengthy one on the Spanish playwright, Calderón. This essay is a review of a book of translations *The Dramas of Calderón,* by Denis Florence McCarthy, a Dublin writer and contributor to *The Nation,* published by Dolman in London in 1853. Jane Wilde's review essay is much more than an account of McCarthy's translations of six Calderón plays, being built around a profound and detailed knowledge of the Spanish dramatist's life and plays, and a shrewd analysis of the texture of Spanish writing in the seventeenth century. Jane Wilde makes the point that 'the Arabs held Spain from the eighth to the fifteenth century.'[42] She sees this eastern influence as beneficial and fruitful to Calderón and making his imagination, in her word, 'oriental'. She provides a close reading of each play, including *The Purgatory of St Patrick,* set in Ireland. Jane Wilde may have known the translator of the volume, but this doesn't mean that her review is a positive one, rather she uses her technical knowledge of meter as a poet to conclude that his translation of Calderón is 'unfortunate,' in terms of the emphasis he has created and the ways in which he has rendered the Spanish metre into English. Indeed, her overall sense is that McCarthy may have failed in his endeavour to render the poetry of Calderón's dramas into English because it simply cannot be done. It is an entertaining essay and one that convinces the reader of Jane Wilde's perceptive scholarly knowledge of Calderón's plays.

Her own Irish interests are apparent in her essay on Swift in which she chooses to concentrate on the lives of Stella and Vanessa, Swift's two partners, Esther Johnson, (1681–1728) and Esther Van Homrigh (1688–1723). Her firm belief was that women,

---

42. Ibid., p. 54.

in general, are incapable of genius and this is a tragic occurrence because they are consequently excluded from the pantheon of greatness and literary achievement. This is one of Jane Wilde's outstanding essays, readable, passionate, well-informed and with her own very particular view of the relationship between genius and mortals, and between men and women, Swift himself is a figure she admires and with whom she identifies. She recounts the course of his slow and difficult rise to fame and influence, and his unrelenting integrity:

> He refused to become chaplain to Lord Oxford, then Prime Minister, and in a letter to Bolingbroke writes: "I would have you to know, Sir, that if the Queen gave you a dukedom and the Garter to-morrow, with the Treasury staff at the end of it, I'd regard you no more than if you were not worth a groat." This is the true Republican spirit that actuates Genius in all ages. Swift would not allow intellect even in another to descend a step from the height where God had placed it.[43]

Her focus is on the tortured relationship between Swift and the two women who loved him, and her theory on the nature of genius again surfaces here. It occurs elsewhere in her writings and again, it is the sense that the most creative natures are the least capable of reciprocating passion and empathy:

> It is a truth, however, of all natures gifted with genius, that they are the least capable of constant, concentrated love. They live in the Infinite; in lofty purposes and grand deeds, of which humanity at large is the object. They can throw their hearts into a cause, but not yield it to an individual. What isolated human heart is vast enough to absorb their

---

43. Ibid., p. 278.

affections or satisfy their aspirations? Souls like theirs cannot have free action within so limited a horizon. What they call love is a sublime adoration for an idol robed in the fleeting colours of the imagination; but the delusion cannot last, and the society of minds inferior to their own often becomes in the end either wearisome or disgusting.[44]

Her final conclusion was that both women were victims and tragic ones at that, shut out of the possibility of genius and therefore doomed to unhappiness:

Two more female hearts are added to the pile laid upon the altar of unhappy love. Is it so strange a fate? Is not love ever the sole tragedy of a woman's destiny? Stella and Vanessa at least have won a glory to gild the gloom of fate denied to many; for the name of their lover is a catafalque whereon they lie in state for the tender sorrow of all ages, with the asbestos torch of his genius illuminating the bier.[45]

Very different is her essay on the English writer Harriet Martineau (1802–1876) and her *Literary Celebrities,* in which she sees the increasing influence and power of women writers in contemporary Britain as proof of a more enlightened society. Yet, Jane Wilde finds that, in her writings on figures like Lord Palmerston, the historian McCauley, Byron and many others 'Miss Martineau's judgements are indeed for the most part cruel scathing and remorseless,'[46] but goes on to comment that 'Still the biographies are worth preserving.' She believed that Martineau had too much contact with these well-known men and women and found that her familiarity made her too liable to undermine and denigrate them. One of the few men that Martineau praised was George

---

44. Ibid., p. 142.
45. Ibid., p. 147.
46. Ibid., p. 113.

Howard, Lord Carlisle (1802–1864), the Lord Lieutenant of Ireland who had conferred his knighthood on William Wilde in his wife's presence; here we find Jane Wilde agreeing with Martineau and calling him 'amiable and gifted.'[47]

She returns to Ireland in her review of a biography of Marguerite, Lady Blessington (1798–1849) by Richard Madden. Jane Wilde finds much to admire in the woman who was forced to flee from London after years at the pinnacle of literary society, in debt to the tune of one hundred thousand pounds and yet with the resolve to remake her life. Born in Tipperary, as Marguerite Power, she was one of three sisters who became countesses. For many years, she had been a successful writer, a friend of Byron in Italy and author of an important book about him, and the host of a literary and political salon in Gore House in the most fashionable part of London. Jane Wilde's essay is one of great admiration for her style. What Jane Wilde found most impressive was Marguerite Blessington's response to the sudden loss of her wealth and status, after years of overspending: 'At sixty years of age she found herself a fugitive in Paris, youth, beauty, wealth, prestige, magnificence all gone. By this she strove to build up another future, already she planned new works of literature and new modes of life.'[48] The parallels with her own life were clear, although Jane Wilde herself was fortunate to survive in London for twenty years, while Marguerite Blessington died seven weeks after her flight from London.

No such admiration is shown in her essay on George Eliot. In this essay, Jane Wilde acknowledges Eliot's many achievements and the fact that she 'exacts homage from all the leading men.'[49] This status is underpinned by economic success and Jane Wilde sees money earned by writing as one of the key factors in the recognition of the status of women writers:

---

47. Ibid., p. 117.
48. Ibid., p. 151.
49. Ibid., p. 171.

She achieved also an unexampled financial success. No other woman, perhaps, of her generation realised forty thousand pounds by writing. And she deserved it, for she strove earnestly to perfect her work, though often in the effort to seem wise she attained only to being dull. Yet "Romola" is a great book to add to literature; sufficient to ensure lasting fame to the author, even had she written nothing else; but in "Daniel Deronda" and several of her later works she enforces her views with rather too much wearisome prolixity and assertive dogmatism.[50]

Jane Wilde has no hesitation in questioning the reputation of the leading writer of her time: 'Why cannot English novelists see the superior force, beauty, and power of the French style of writing, where a line, a word, is made to unfold a character or express a dramatic situation, and the line or word reveals more of both in a sudden flash than all the long-winded descriptive sentences of English writers, with their numerous clauses and concatenations?'[51] At the same time, she is unrelenting in her attack on Eliot's sermonising, her desire to teach the reader and the ways in which she obstructs her own narrative.

The Right Reverend Dr Doyle was a reforming bishop who promoted the idea of national school education in early nineteenth-century Ireland. He is the subject of her short essay on the life of James Warren Doyle (1788–1834) and her approval of his work is seen in her statement that 'Both Bishop Doyle and Daniel O'Connell were the great central figures of the Emancipation era and equally powerful, though their tactics were different. O'Connell's cry rallying cry was 'Agitate!' Dr Doyle's was 'Educate!''[52]

In her essay on the fiction of Benjamin Disraeli again she takes

---

50. Ibid., p. 171.
51. Ibid., p. 176.
52. Ibid., p. 198.

on a leading figure in British letters and politics but is even-handed in the way she defends him against the critical attacks that tore his novel *Endymion* apart, partly because he was prime minister: 'Why should it be necessary for all the critics to rush at once upon a book and tear the heart and life out of it and then flight it dead upon the shelf, to be named and thought of no more?'[53] Her survey of the novel is judicious in that she admires certain aspects of the book, drawing out the real life personages that Disraeli used, like the Princess of Wales and the Empress Eugénie, but was nonetheless honest in discussing the imaginative difficulties and shortcomings of the novel. As she saw it, much of Disraeli's writing in *Endymion* was without dramatic energy, creating protagonists that are often standing in for broad generalised types rather than fully-realised imagined individuals. She shrewdly suggests that the real interest for most Victorian readers in his novel comes from the elements that reflect Disraeli's own fascinating life, treating fiction as veiled autobiography and thus able to glean a great deal of information about public life and figures. Ultimately, she sees the novel as a missed opportunity, weakened by a sense of gloom perhaps caused by political defeat and failing health, and her final judgement is 'The Semitic aspirations would thus have been satisfied, and genius and ambition, Endymion and Myra might rest content with their mission in the world and their place in history'.[54]

Her undiminished enthusiasm for Thomas Moore is seen in her extensive essay on his poetry where she celebrates the fact that

> Translations of the "Melodies" were rapidly made into all the tongues of Europe. Wherever oppression existed, they helped to give resistance utterance. They passed from nation to nation, as a burning torch passes from hand to hand, the signal of the uprising of a people against tyranny; and so, they exist an enduring portion of the world's heritage, graven

---

53. Ibid., p. 231.
54. Ibid., p. 220.

with a diamond pen upon the rocks for ever. The enthusiasm kindled by them in Ireland alarmed the Government. Their tendency was pronounced "mischievous," and the idea was entertained of forcibly suppressing their publication. Moore had to defend himself against the charge of "stirring up the passions of a turbulent mob."[55]

The rest of *Notes on Men, Women, and Books* covers the work of such writers as Leigh Hunt, Wordsworth and the Poet Laureate, Alfred Tennyson. Her detailed reading of Tennyson's poem 'The Princess' is filled with admiration of a poet she dubs 'a true poet priest, one who has entered within the veil,'[56] yet she finds too little empathy in his celebrated 'In Memoriam.'[57] Her admiration for Wordsworth, and the clarity and precision of her close readings of his poems makes her essay on his work one of the strongest in the collection. She opens with this majestic endorsement of his achievements: 'Wordsworth's long life was not passed in vain for humanity. As an apostle of the Divine, a light bringer to his age, leading many souls upwards from darkness to the serene harmony of the higher spiritual life, the great poet nobly fulfilled his mission and left the impress of his genius indelibly stamped on the literature of his country.'[58] Jane Wilde's own poetic credo, the notion of the search for the divine and the higher spiritual life in the creation of verse, is never clearer than here and constitutes a revelation of her own sense of what poetry could achieve.

Notes on Men, Women, and Books concludes with an essay called 'World Leaders,' a previously-published review of a long poem called 'Time in Dreamland' by John Frazer Corkran. Born in Dublin in 1808, he became a journalist, worked in Paris as a correspondent, and died in 1884. Jane Wilde may have known

---

55. Ibid., p. 187.
56. Ibid., p. 290.
57. Ibid., p. 320.
58. Ibid., p. 247.

him as a fellow-contributor to *The Dublin Magazine* and Henriette Corkran, whose *Celebrities and I* (1902),[59] mentions spending time with Jane Wilde, was his daughter. His other daughter was the writer Alice Corkran (1843–1916). Jane Wilde's essay explores Corkran's work and argues that 'The subject is the history of the great soul of humanity itself considered in its unity – its moral evolution.'[60] She goes on to comment that 'With such an ambitious subject, the scope nonetheless seems to have been exclusively male, Raphael, Michelangelo, and the style admired by the author is never beneath his either his subject or his purpose. In every line, there is the inspiration of a calm, noble, reflective mind.'[61]

The poem ranges from Renaissance Italy to Reformation Germany, and from the battles of the Counter-Reformation to the formation of the Jesuits. On the basis of her account and with copious use of quotes from the text, it seems that 'Time in Dreamland', was a (slightly tiresome) polemical reading of early modern European history that pitted the deviousness of Catholic powers like the Valois in France and the Hapsburgs in Spain against the truth and the heroism of Protestants like William the Silent and of the English rulers of the time. It is surprising that Jane Wilde should have found such a profoundly anti-Catholic text so empathetic, but her interest was in the form and in the ways in which poetry could have the ambition to encompass the progress of history and the clash of religions and of cultures, despite the apparently broad strokes of Corkran's ideological interests in the poem.

The collection concludes with her review of a performance by the Irish-born actor Charles Kean (1811–1868) in his performance as Richard III. Her knowledge of Victorian stagecraft is impressive here and her interest in Shakespeare evident. Jane Wilde wrote about this character, whose ferocity and total self-absorption she

---

59. Henriette Corkran, *Celebrities and I* (London: Hutchinson, 1902).
60. *Men, Women and Books*, p. 326.
61. Ibid., p. 329.

admired, in precise and striking language: 'We hold our breath, we shudder at the stroke that is to doom this colossal force to annihilation. One looks for portents when he dies. His place is vacant on earth as Lucifer's in heaven.'[62] She had nothing but praise for Kean himself and saw his performance in these terms: 'Never was there more perfect sympathy established between author, actor and audience, they seemed to form together one mighty human mind – one 'over soul', all individual feeling was absorbed in the common sympathetic emotion that made each feel with the aggregated intensity of all.'[63] Where and when she actually saw him perform is not clear, as his last professional engagement was in Liverpool in 1867, but she may have seen him on the London stage at the Princess Theatre where he performed Richard III in the late 1850s, during one of her visits, or on her way to Sweden.

Social Studies (1893)

Published in 1893 by Ward and Downey, this lively collection of her published articles includes two new translated stories, 'The Two Artists' from the Spanish and 'Tertia Mors Est' from the German. The range of her interests here are focussed on societal norms and conventions and she looks at themes like 'Social Graces', 'Suitability of Dress', 'The Destiny of Humanity.' Often these are based on her published journal articles, like 'Australia – a Plea for Emigration' 'and The Vision of the Vatican' and she draws on her own life, 'Irish Leaders and Martyrs'.

Social Studies opens with 'The Bondage of Women' and in this essay, Jane Wilde articulates her feminist beliefs when she protests the ongoing social and economic repression of women. She opens with an historical survey of the condition of women in many cultures and laments the deeply disturbing fact that, as she says, 'the history of women has been a mournful record of

---

62. Jane Wilde, *Social Studies*, p. 349.
63. Ibid., p. 325.

helpless resignation to social prejudice and legal tyranny.'[64] This lively and impassioned sweep through history includes an account of patriarchal societies and religious beliefs both Christian and Buddhist, ancient Egypt and Greece and the misogyny of witch hunting and killings and she concludes that 'We have now traced the history of women from Paradise to the nineteenth century and have heard nothing through the long roll of ages but the clank of their fetters.'[65] She applauds the hidden history of feminist political thought throughout the ages but, in many ways, replicated some of this patriarchal thought when she says, 'The love of woman is generally aspiration – hero worship; while man receives homage more readily that he gives it.'[66] But Jane Wilde also argues that such a resignation of a woman's autonomy to her husband's rule and command needs to be revised and remade and draws on the lessons of early Christianity to promote the idea of equality. Christianity as Jane Wilde interprets it allowed for a kind of power balance between men and women. Her lament is also for the lack of honours and rewards for achievements that many Victorian women suffered under, while always contributing to the economy in every way. Furthermore, she asks: 'The Queen has already founded an order for distinguished bravery…would it not be worthy of her sex and station to institute a royal order of merit for women eminent in literature and art, with title and life income,'[67] thus anticipating Virginia Woolf's call for five hundred pounds a year and a room of one's own for the female writer. She also called for women to teach in universities and deplores the fact that 'Female education at present is mere dilettantism.'[68] She wants to see women as colonial governors and in positions of real political influence: 'Some noble purpose, some grand sphere,

---

64. Ibid., p. 1.
65. Ibid., p. 13.
66. Ibid., p. 15.
67. Ibid., p. 20.
68. Ibid., p. 21.

where passionate energy can work along with duty, will ensure these lofty missionary natures the only happiness of which such exalted organisations are susceptible.'[69]

Right after this direct and clearly-defined feminist essay comes 'Genius and Marriage', a curious and often contradictory interpretation of the gendered nature of genius and the domestic world as the enemy of true, unbridled creativity. This theme occurs elsewhere in her essays and reviews and sits uneasily with her championing of the rights of women and the need for equality. She takes as her example the views of the French novelist, Alphonse Daudet (1840–1897), who believed that 'the marriage state is quite detrimental to the highest intellectual life and mars its development.'[70] Jane Wilde hurries to exempt Daudet's own wife, Julia Allard Daudet (1844–1940), a poet and one of the first readers of Proust, from this patriarchal dismissal, but the main drift of the essay is to the effect that 'the daughters of men who wed with the sons of gods should have the courage to face the lightnings and the thunders, if they dare to stand on the mountain height with an immortal husband.'[71] The essay is filled with examples of men of creative genius who betrayed their artistic calling by marrying women of distressingly bourgeois mediocrity, all set on domestic life and destroying the flame of their husband's intellect. Her account of the life of Jane Welsh Carlyle, wife of the much-admired Thomas Carlyle (1801–1866), stings: 'She ought to have considered that her existence was really of no importance to the universe but her husband's words and works had power to send the world on its path of progress with mighty tangential force and to drive a current of new life into the heart of the century. He was necessary to humanity; but she was only necessary to smooth the path his soul travelled.'[72]

---

69. Ibid., p. 27.
70. Ibid., p. 28.
71. Ibid., p. 31.
72. Ibid., p. 49.

How did Jane Wilde reconcile her feminism with such a narrow view of the creative potential of her contemporaries? The answer is that she doesn't. The contrast between these two essays is profound. The first is a scholarly account of the subordinate position held by women throughout many cultures and the second a patriarchal belief in the lack of true genius: 'A woman is so easily replaced in the vast working world of life but a great man's throne is vacant for evermore.'[73] Jane Wilde did hold these apparently contradictory positions. Like many Victorian men and women, she both questioned normative gender assumptions and embodied them, investing the vocation of poetry with male authority.

In her remaining essays, she always seeks out examples of the ways in which women can assert their equality, as in her writing on American women. 'Social Graces' is a meditation on the manners and on the role of social abilities and behaviour in bettering the public sphere and all of her examples are drawn from women writers and their abilities to transform their societies by their modes of behaviour. It is a learned and intellectually well-informed essay on a slightly vague topic and one which makes puzzling generalisations like this: 'Women live so far apart from practical life that their opinion on any grave deep subject is really worth nothing but the sympathy of a woman is worth everything to a cause or a human heart.'[74]

Jane Wilde's own day by day encounters with practical life, like paying her rent and gaining income from her writings is evident from her letters, and the learning that underpins her literary essays is deep and grave yet she acquiesces with the standard Victorian dismissal of women as outside the demands and the harsh realities of economic and political life. Jane Wilde recounts the way in which Byron's wife, Anne Isabelle Noel (1792–1860), asked her husband if she was interrupting him while writing and he responded, 'Damnably', an angry and churlish response that Jane

73. Ibid., p. 51.
74. Ibid., p. 66.

Wilde approved of. The right woman, tactful and subservient, can improve her world and her society, but, this essay argues, the wrong woman can irritate and annoy because she asserts herself. The next essay, 'Venus Victrix', continues this theme and opens with the idea that 'Woman lies at the basis of all life, whether for good or evil.'[75] This essay celebrates what Jane Wilde perceived to be the nobility of the female character, the fact that a woman's heart will rule over the woman's brain and that intellectual achievement is a male preserve, with female support.

A less contradictory essay is her account of the spiritual affinity between a man and a woman. The Prussian philosopher, Wilhelm von Humboldt (1767–1835), was the author of a book called *Letters to a Lady*, published after his death in 1847, consisting of letters to Charlotte Diede (1769–1846), with whom he had had a brief platonic love affair in his youth and whom he supported financially for many years. Jane Wilde herself had such a lifelong correspondence with John Hilson and regarded the affinity between Humboldt and Diede as a rarefied and spiritually-uplifting one: 'The inner spiritual life is developed more truthfully and purely in woman than in man, for men grow hard and selfish and crabbed by the dull routine of work laid on them where the toil is not lightened by love. While toil, no matter how arduous, is borne cheerfully by a wife or mother for the sake of those she loves and often without any recompense.'[76] This essay ends on a high note, seeing non-sexualised affinity between a man and a woman as eternal and harmonious and, most importantly, equal. This balance is also to be seen in her essay on 'Suitability of Dress', where she rehearses the historical development of clothing in a number of cultures and calls for a simplification of dress and of social manners to allow a greater ease and comfort for women and an ending of the constrictions of female codes of dressing. Jane Wilde was a supporter of the campaign for rational dress for

---

75. Ibid., p. 78.
76. Ibid., p. 103.

women and her daughter in law Constance wore some of the more 'revolutionary' clothes that allowed for comfort and a lessening of tight and dangerous corsets.

'American Women' reflected her lifelong interest in a country where her work was celebrated, especially in Irish-American communities. Although she never went there, many of her acquaintances in London were American, and from this she drew her opinions:

> The women express their ideas with firmness, precision, and perfect self-possession, and are admirable speakers on the platform. The American woman, on the contrary, disdains this colourless uniformity, and revolts against social usages that would limit her bold originality and assertive self-manifestation. She is proud, conscious, strong-souled, and self-reliant. "I am an American girl" is answer enough to any timid old-world bigot. And this phrase expresses at once dignity, courage, self-respect, and the independence of the emancipated republican.[77]

The energy of this essay is refreshing after some of her pronouncements on the gendered nature of genius and the passive goodness of the female influence on male identity. Her idea of the American female temperament is a lively, assertive and attractive one:

> But the vigorous, vivacious American girl never omits a syllable; she speaks in a loud, clear voice, as if for the reporters, and as one worth hearing, who demands and extorts attention. She accentuates all she says with firm purpose and resolute determination to be heard. She is sharp, smart, and terrible at repartee, and may, perhaps, be

---

77. Ibid., p. 131.

sometimes fatiguing to the English ear with her voluble flow of words. The English girl never stares, nor asks questions with obtrusive curiosity. She is trained to seem and to be a negation – a dormant soul without volition or an opinion on any subject, felt or expressed. Her American cousin, however, has an aggressive frankness, based chiefly upon interrogatories and bold personalities. Her gaze is clear and direct; not "the stony British stare," but with the large, truthful eyes of childhood – the eager, inquiring glance of a candid nature. Truth is in all her words.'[78]

Although she had never visited the United States, Jane Wilde makes this essay something of a travelogue as well and she evaluates cities like Boston, 'A city of advanced intellects and the emancipated woman', Philadelphia, 'The Quaker City', and Washington, 'grand and stately.'[79] She draws on contemporary fiction to discuss the archetypes of Englishness that predominate in American fiction and celebrates the literary representation of the emancipated woman, probably bearing in mind women like Frances Hodgson Burnett (1849–1924), the author of *The Secret Garden* and *Little Lord Fauntleroy*, who visited her salon, Mrs Frank Leslie, her former daughter-in-law, and her friend Anna, Countess de Brémont when she makes these statements:

> Women in America, whether married or single, rule society, and do not suffer society to rule them. They carry all before them with imperial sway and are the beautiful despots of the land. Fathers, brothers and husbands are at work all day in the fierce strife and excitement of the ceaseless speculation, which is the national form of gambling. But the men never interfere with the interior management of the house; all the arrangements and expenditure and machinery of social life

---

78. Ibid., p. 131.
79. Ibid., p. 134.

are left to the taste, judgment and discretion of the wife. The province of the husband is merely to fling down the showers of gold, which the fascinating better half spends right royally.[80]

She sees the puritan legacy in the adherence to directness and truth in American women and celebrates what she sees as the importance of the Irish strain in the making of the American melting pot: 'The Saxon basis is the rough block of the nation; but it is the Celtic influence that gives it all its artistic value and finish.'[81] And she adds that America has protected Irish exiles, fleeing, it is implied, from British rule and British injustice. She ends with admiring comments on the advance of women's rights, with American women at the front of this struggle, and celebrates the future for feminism there.

'Australia – A Plea for Emigration' is her review essay of a book on Australia by the Irish born John Leslie Fitzgerald Foster (1818–1900), Colonial Secretary for Victoria. Here Jane Wilde praises the achievements of colonial rule in Australia, the natural beauty of the continent, its resources and wealth, and advocates mass emigration as the solution for poverty and overcrowding in Britain. Her argument has a particular force when she makes a strong case for Australia as an answer to Ireland's woes: 'And why above all, should the force and fire of Irish manhood be wasted in vain, complaints that their people are 'the worst fed, the worst houses, the worst clothed, the most utterly destitute of any of the nations of the earth,' (which is indeed a sad truth) when they could arise and go forth to a noble and splendid heritage.'[82] Her belief in emigration as a solution to Irish poverty is also underpinned with an attack on the mismanagement of Irish affairs by the British, and she makes a pointed comparison with the excellent good sense of

---

80. Ibid., pp. 130–131.
81. Ibid., p. 135.
82. Ibid., p. 223.

Australian colonial governance. She also includes the veiled threat that in future, Irish-Australians will contribute to the cause of Irish freedom and be as powerful a lobby as the Irish-Americans. Her call to her fellow Irish men and women to seek 'the fair and fertile land' of Australia is as much an attack on British rule and the many economic mistakes made by the British in Ireland.

The range of essays continues with a close reading of Victor Hugo's 1878 poem 'Le Pape,' a poem in which Hugo imagines an unnamed Pope tormented by a dream in which all of the rulers and kings of the world come to him in a vision and the pope is appalled at their arrogance, thirst for war and lack of humility. In response, in his dream, the pope articulates a vision of the real basis for Christianity, and Jane Wilde admires this closing moment greatly, calling it 'this divine dream of a noble soul filled with pity for the wrongs of man.'[83] Her willingness to engage with scientific subjects can be seen in her essay, 'The Destiny of Humanity', where she reviews the writings of Richard Anthony Proctor, (1830–1888) a popular astronomer, and the author of a series of well received guides to the planets. 'The Poet as Teacher' was the essay where her own poetic vocation is to the fore and in which she reveals a great deal about her own sense of the aesthetic role and function of poetry in society:

> 'It is one of Goethe's profound aphorisms, that "Every day we should in some way renew our impression of the true and the beautiful by a verse from some great poet, the sight of a painting or a statue, or by a noble thought from some heroic mind; for the spiritual within is ever in danger for being choked and suffocated by the rank luxuriance of the weeds and thorns that crowd our daily life." In this country, however, Art has but few temples wherein lessons of grace and beauty can be taught the people; nor can even the glorious

---

83. Ibid., p. 265.

book of Nature be enjoyed by those who, with toiling hands and ever lowered eyes, workday, and night at the loom of life to earn the scanty bread of subsistence.'[84]

Her collection was well received except for *The Athenaeum* which said 'It was a clever set of essays, not with much substance.'[85]

By 1894, Willie and his second wife Lily were living in Oakley Street with Jane Wilde and she had come to appreciate the good qualities of her new daughter-in-law, while her son's health continued to deteriorate. Trials had been a big part of Jane's life and her own reputation was about to suffer in the disaster that now engulfed the Wilde family. Oscar's relationship with Lord Alfred Douglas had enraged his father, the violent Marquis of Queensbury, and finally the tension erupted in a court case where Oscar sued him for libel concerning a calling card Queensbury had left for him at his club, dubbing him a 'somdomite' [sic]. The case for libel was not proven and instead, Oscar was arrested and tried for gross indecency. He was then sentenced to two years hard labour, declared bankrupt and his wife and sons left England for exile in Switzerland. These 1895 trials of her son Oscar were a point of great difficulty for Jane Wilde herself, but her loyalty to him throughout was unwavering. They had worked together so closely in London in their various literary projects and he had been generous and supportive, while Willie's addiction and his financial struggles had impoverished her.

Many critics and writers wondered afterward why Oscar Wilde had taken such a dangerous case, when it exposed him to the risk of imprisonment and disgrace. In some narratives, Jane Wilde herself, with her experience in court rooms was cast as the main influence behind Oscar's decision, after his first trial, to stay on in the Cadogan Hotel. By staying in London, he was forced to face arrest and imprisonment for gross indecency, despite been

---

84. Ibid., p. 273.
85. Melville, p. 236.

given a chance by the police to flee to France. W.B. Yeats wrote in his 1914 autobiographies that 'I heard later, from whom I forget now, that Lady Wilde had said: 'If you stay, even if you go to prison, you will always be my son, it will make no difference to my affection but if you go, I will never speak to you again.'[86] This was to damage her posthumous reputation, casting her as reckless and intent on conflict, prepared to allow her son to sacrifice his safety for a gesture of melodramatic self-assertion. There is no other independent evidence of her making such a declaration, and Oscar had been the sole source of financial support to her in her recent difficulties. What is known is that she stayed loyal to him. When all hotels in London were closed to him when he lost the libel case against Queensbury, Jane Wilde made him welcome in her home in Oakley Street.

Two more trials took place and Oscar was eventually sentenced to two years hard labour and was made to serve every day of that sentence. After the trial, Jane Wilde stayed in correspondence with Constance, who was forced to flee the country and to change her name and that of her sons. Jane Wilde wrote to her in April 1895 to say that 'I am poorly and utterly miserable. I do not like the idea of the boys changing their names. It would bring them much confusion. But at all events wait till the trial is over.'[87] Some well-wishers had sent Oscar one thousand pounds and from this, his friends paid for her rent in Oakley Street, but she had little money otherwise. She lamented the fact that he didn't write to her and all visitors were refused entrance. When Willie's daughter Dorothy was born in 1895, Oscar's money paid the medical expenses and all money sent to her had to be kept hidden from Willie.

Jane Wilde had an attack of bronchitis in January 1896 and asked for Oscar to be sent for. This was refused and she died 3rd February without seeing him again. Only Willie and his wife Lily attended the funeral, and her grave in Kensal Green is now lost, as

---

86. W. B. Yeats, *Autobiographies* (New York: Senate Books, 1995), p. 278.
87. Tipper, *Lady Wilde's Letters to Constance,* p. 37.

the headstone was never paid for. Later, her great-grandson Merlin Holland arranged for a plaque to be added to William Wilde's grave in Mount Jerome cemetery in Dublin. *The Times* of 7th February called her 'a distinguished member of the Young Ireland party, of virile and passionate rhetoric.' *The Athenaeum* said, 'under the mask of brilliant display and bohemian recklessness lay a deep and loyal soul and a kindly and sympathetic nature.' As far away as Virginia, *The Virginia Enterprise* called her 'A brilliant woman who had contributed so much to literature and social life in England and Ireland.'[88] All of this praise was given even though her son's reputation was now in ruins and he had become a byword for sexual scandal. Oscar believed that she had come to his cell the night she died to say goodbye and his wife Constance travelled from Geneva to break the news, knowing how it would grieve him and indeed fearing it would kill him. Willie, despite his addiction and his bad health (his own death was imminent), wrote of his mother as 'the best, truest and most loyal friend I had on earth. Her end was perfect peace. She was quite conscious up to an hour before her passing.'[89]

---

88. *Virginia Enterprise,* 10th April 1896, p. 2.
89. Fitzsimons, p. 376.

Conclusion

Apart from her Irish legends and superstitions and some of her Famine poetry, Jane Wilde's writings disappeared from print soon after her death. Critical neglect was compounded by the fact that her posthumous reputation was destroyed by her perceived association with her son's shamed sexual identity and downfall. All throughout the twentieth century in her own country and in Oscar Wilde biographies, she was seen as a figure to be ridiculed. Now, two hundred years after her birth, a scholarly reassessment is taking place and this study, along with the outstanding work of Karen Tipper, Eleanor Fitzsimons and Emer O'Sullivan, reveals the dynamic relationship contemporary criticism has with her ideas and her aesthetics. Slowly a critical appreciation of the range and the depth of her writing has been re-established within reclamations of Irish women's writing in the nineteenth century. Jane Wilde's writings and her career offer us an insight into the rewarding complexities and contradictions of Victorian feminism.

Much scholarly work remains to be done on Jane Wilde's writings. To date, there is no contemporary edition of her poetry, little critical consideration of her translations and her travel writing, and the scope and insights in her essays are largely unknown to contemporary scholars, feminists and readers. Her links with France, intellectually and aesthetically, would reward scholarly attention, as would her writings on American women and on the Irish-American. Her work is key to the formulation of an Irish cultural nationalist identity, an identity that shaped the path to Irish independence, and the new Ireland that was to neglect and trivialise her. The aim of this study is to highlight the depth of her scholarship and her creativity and to recognise how valuable her writing is, a body of work lost in the fissures of the Irish literary canon until now. Jane Wilde's voice is one worth listening to.

Bibliography

Jane Wilde: Primary Works.

Sidonia (London: Reeves and Turner, 1849).
Pictures of the First French Revolution (London: Simms and McIntyre, 1850).
The Wanderer and his Home (London: Simms and McIntyre, 1851).
The Glacier Land (London: Simms and McIntyre, 1852).
The First Temptation (London: Cautley Newby, 1863).
Poems by Speranza (Dublin: James Duffy, 1864).
Memoir of Gabriel Beranger with William Wilde (Dublin: Gill, 1880).
Driftwood from Scandinavia (London: Richard Bentley, 1884).
Ancient Legends, Mystic Charms, and Superstitions of Ireland (London: Ward & Downey, 1887).
Ancient Cures, Charms and Usages of Ireland (London: Ward & Downey, 1890).
Notes on Men and Women and Books (London: Ward & Downey, 1891).
Social Studies (London: Ward & Downey, 1893).

Secondary Criticism

Campbell, Matthew. 'Poetry, 1845–90' in *A History of Modern Irish Women's Writing*, eds. Clíona Ó'Gallchoir and Heather Ingman (Cambridge: Cambridge University Press, 2018).
Coakley, Davis. *Oscar Wilde: The Importance of Being Irish* (Dublin: Townhouse, 1994).
Colman, Anne. 'Far from Silent: Nineteenth-Century Irish Women Writers' in *Gender Perspectives in Nineteenth-Century Ireland: Public and Private Spheres, Society for the Study of Nineteenth Century Ireland 2*, eds. Margaret Kelleher and James H. Murphy (Dublin: Irish Academic Press, 1997), pp. 203–217.
Corkran, Henriette. *Celebrities and I* (London: Hutchinson, 1902).
Cronin, Michael. 'Lady Jane "Speranza" Wilde and the Translator's Invisibility,' *Claritas* 8 (2002), pp. 83–102.

Deane, Seamus. 'Poetry and Song 1800–1890' in *The Field Day Anthology of Irish Writing*, vol. 2, edited by Seamus Deane et al. (Derry: Field Day, 1991).
De Brémont, Anna. *Oscar Wilde and His Mother, A Memoir* (London: Everett, 1914).
De Vere White, Terence. *The Parents of Oscar Wilde* (London: Hodder & Stoughton, 1967).
Fitzsimons, Eleanor. *Wilde's Women* (London: Duckworth, 2015).
Gavan Duffy, Charles. *My Life in Two Hemispheres* (New York: McMillan, 1898).
Harris, Frank. *Oscar Wilde* (Dorset Press: New York, 1989).
Howe, Marjorie. '"Tears and Blood": Lady Wilde and the Emergence of an Irish Cultural Nationalism,' in *Ideology and Ireland in the Nineteenth Century*, ed. Tadhg Foley and Seán Ryder (Dublin: Four Courts, 1998) pp 54–76.
Killeen, Jarlath. *The Faiths of Oscar Wilde* (Hampshire: Palgrave, 2005).
___. *The Fairy Tales of Oscar Wilde* (London: Ashgate, 2007).
Lambert, Eric. *Mad with Much Heart* (London: Muller, 1967).
Martin, Amy 'The Skeleton at the Feast: Lady Wilde's Famine Poetry and Irish Internationalist Critiques of Food Scarcity,' in *Women and the Great Hunger,* ed. Christine Kinealy, Jason King, and Ciaran Reilly (Hamden, CT: Quinnipiac University Press, 2017), p 151.
Melville, Joy. *Mother of Oscar: The Life of Jane Francesca Wilde* (London: John Murray 1994).
Morash, Christopher. *Writing the Irish Famine* (Clarendon Press: Oxford, 1995)
Muir, Jean. '"Speranza" and "Gurth", Jane Francesca Elgee's "unknown Scottish friend"', *The Wildean* No. 21 (July 2002), pp. 2–14.
Novak, Rose. 'Reviving "Eva" of "The Nation?": Eva O'Doherty's Young Ireland Newspaper Poetry' *Victorian Periodicals Review*, Vol. 45, No. 4 (Winter 2012).
Ní Chuilleanáin, Eiléan, *The Wilde Legacy* (Dublin: Four Courts Press, 2003).
Ó'Gallchoir, Clíona and Heather Ingman. *A History of Modern Irish Women's Literature.* (Cambridge: Cambridge University Press, 2018).
O'Sullivan, Emer. *The Fall of the House of Wilde* (London: Bloomsbury, 2016).
Read, Charles A ed., *The Cabinet of Irish Literature,* vol iv (London: Blackie and Son 1880),
Ryder, Seán, ed. *James Clarence Mangan: Selected Writings* (Dublin: University College Dublin Press, 2004).
Tipper, Karen. *Lady Jane Wilde's Letters to Fröken Lotten von Kræmer, 1857–1885.* (New York: Edwin Mellen, 2008).
___. *Lady Jane Wilde's Letters to Mr John Hilson 1847–1876* (New York: Mellen, 2010).
___. *Lady Jane Wilde's Letters to Oscar Wilde, 1875–1895* (New York: Mellen, 2011).
___. *Lady Jane Wilde's Letters to Constance Wilde, Friends, and Acquaintances* (New York: Mellen, 2013).
___. *A Critical Biography of Jane Wilde* (New York: Edwin Mellen, 2013).
Tóibín, Colm. *Love in a Dark Time: Gay Lives from Wilde to Almodóvar* (London: Picador 2002).

___. *Mad, Bad and Dangerous to Know* (London: Viking, 2018).
Walshe, Eibhear. *Oscar's Shadow: Wilde and Modern Ireland* (Cork: Cork University Press, 2011).
___. *The Diary of Mary Travers* (Bantry: Somerville Press, 2014).
___. *Selected Writings of Speranza and William Wilde* (Liverpool: Liverpool University Press, 2020).
Weintraub, Stanley. *Bernard Shaw, The Playwright and the Pirate* (Gerrard's Cross: Colin Smythe, 1982).
Wyndham, Horace. *Speranza A Biography of Lady Wilde* (London: Boardman, 1952).
Wilde, Oscar. *De Profundis* (Harmondsworth: Penguin, 1986).
Yeats, W. B. *Autobiographies* (New York: Senate Books, 1995).
___. *Letters to the New Island* (Cambridge: Harvard, 1934).

Index

Alighieri, Dante, 3, 13.
Anderson, Hans Christian, 81.
Athenaeum, The, 120.

Brun, John, 84.
Byron, Lord, 4, 22, 141.
Blessington, Lady Margarite, 134.
Bremont De, Anna, 113.

Calderón, Pedro, 14, 131, 14.
Carleton, William, 50, 98–101, 110.
Carlyle, Thomas, 17–19, 131, 141.
Carlyle, Jane Welch, 141.
Corkran, Henrietta, 138.
Cronin, Michael, 29, 63.

Daudet, Alphonse, 141.
Daudet, Julia Allard, 141.
Davis, Thomas, 2, 8, 61.
Deane, Seamus, 30.
Disraeli, Benjamín, 136.
Doody, Noreen, 11.
Dublin University Review, 62.

Duffy, Charles Gavan, 6, 25–26, 28–29, 53, 56, 61.

Eliot, George, 134–5.
'Eve' of *The Nation*, 26, 47–49.
Fawcett, Millicent, 77–78.
Fitzsimons, Eleanor, 9, 32, 151.

Goethe, Johann Wolfgang, 147.
Gonne, Maud, 28.

Hamilton, Catherine, 81, 111.
Harris, Frank, 7.
Herweg, Georg, 19, 88.
Hilson, John, 15–17, 57–8.
Holland, Merlin, 11, 65.

Ingman, Heather, 9.
Irving, St John, 7.

Johnson, Esther, 131–3.

Kant, Emmanuel, 14.
Kean, Charles, 138–9.
Killeen, Jarlath, 121–122.

Lamartine, Alphonse, 1, 26, 27, 64–5, 129.
Lynn, Kathleen, 28.

Martineau, Harriet, 133–4.
Mangan, James Clarence, 31–2, 38, 109.
Meagher, Thomas Francis, 30, 142.
Melville, Joy, 111.
Merrion Square, 1, 11, 67, 115.
Moore, Thomas, 17, 22, 23, 137.
Morash, Christopher, 31–2, 37, 44.
Nation, The, xi, 10, 19, 27, 55–58, 62.
Ni Chuilleanáin, Eilean, 37–8.

Oehlenschlager, Adam, 81.
Olivercrona, Rosalie, 76, 96–112.
Orr, Alexandra, 108.
O'Connell, Daniel, vii, xi, 21–22, 25–6, 39, 58–62.
O'Gallchoir, Cliona, 9.
O'Sullivan, Emer, 9, 17–18, 42, 96, 101, 151.

Pall Mall Gazette, 114.
Parnell, Charles Stewart, 111.

Richter, Jean Paul, 128–9
Roland, Manon, 130.

Shaw, Bernard, 7, 113.

St James Magazine, 111.
Swift, Jonathan, 13, 14, 131–2.

Tóibín, Colm, 10
Tipper, Karen, 10, 33, 45, 55, 58, 64, 151.
Travers, Mary, 91–102.
Travers, Robert, 95.
Tynan, Katherine, 113.

Undine, 81–82.

Van Homrigh, Esther, 131–3.

Walshe, Eibhear
  Oscar's Shadow, 5.
  The Diary of Mary Travers, 9.
White, Terence De Vere, 15.
Wilde, Constance, 61, 113–4, 150.
Wilde, Isola, 97.
Wilde, Jane (Speranza)
  Sidonia, 62–63.
  Poems, 73.
  Gabriel Beranger, 105–106.
  The American Irish, xii, 107.
  Driftwood from Scandinavia, 78–91.
  Ancient Legends, Mystic Charms, and Superstitions of Ireland, 112–122.
  Ancient Cures, Charms and Usages of Ireland, 122–128.
  Notes on Men and Women and Books, 128–139.

INDEX

Social Studies, 139–151.
Wilde, Oscar, 5, 102, 105, 109, 111, 121, 148–9.
Wilde, William, xii, 31, 68–72, 189–91, 102–109, 115, 121, 126.
Wilde, Willie, 105, 109–9, 111, 127, 148–150.
Woolf, Virginia, 140.

Yeats, WB, 6, 32, 67, 113, 120, 121, 126.
Young Irelanders, The, 22, 56.

Titles also available from **EER**

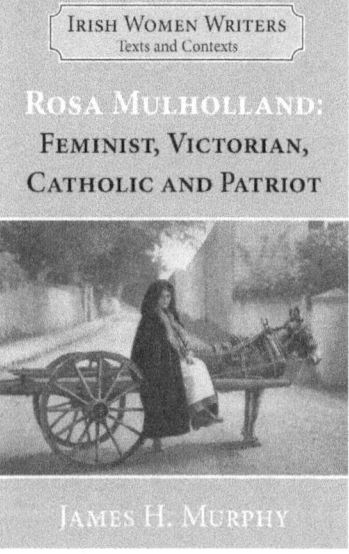

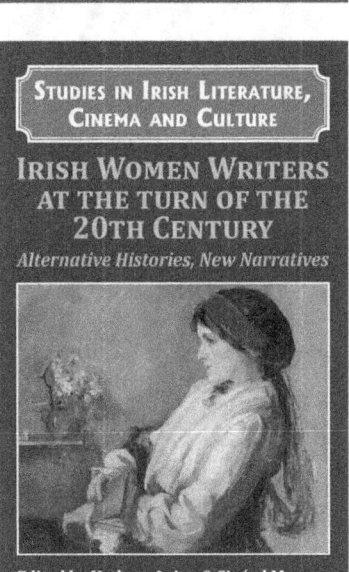
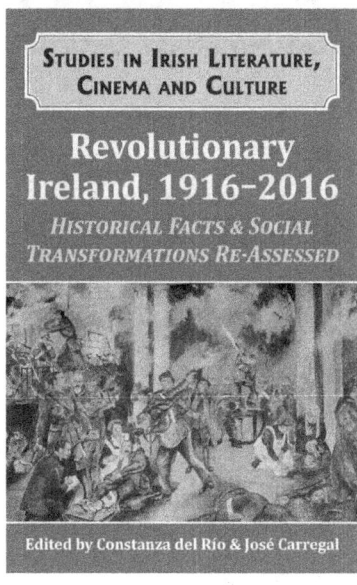

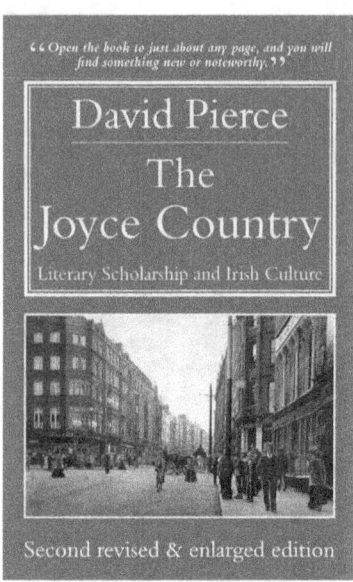

www.ingramcontent.com/pod-product-compliance
Lightning Source LLC
Chambersburg PA
CBHW061449300426
44114CB00014B/1903